# Not Your Mother's Book ...
## On Home Improvement

Created and edited by
Dahlynn McKowen,
Ken McKowen and Pamela Frost

Published by
**Publishing Syndicate**

PO Box 607
Orangevale California 95662
www.PublishingSyndicate.com

# Not Your Mother's Book...
## On Home Improvement

Copyright 2013 by Publishing Syndicate LLC

*We would like to thank the many individuals
who granted us permission to reprint their stories.
See the complete listing beginning on page 320.*

Created and edited by Dahlynn McKowen,
Ken McKowen and Pamela Frost
Cover and book design by Publishing Syndicate
Cover art: Tools © donates1205/Shutterstock.com
Cover art: Paint © Sarunyu_foto/Shutterstock.com

Published by
**Publishing Syndicate**
PO Box 607
Orangevale California 95662

www.PublishingSyndicate.com
www.Facebook.com/PublishingSyndicate
Twitter: @PublishingSynd

Print Edition ISBN: 978-1-938778-12-4
EPUB Digital Edition ISBN: 978-1-938778-13-1
Library of Congress Control Number 2013938827

Printed in Canada

This book is a collaborative effort. Writers from all over the world submitted their work for consideration, with 65 stories being selected.

Publishing Syndicate strongly encourages you to submit your story for one of its many anthologies. You'll find information on how to do so at the end of this book, starting on page 322.

# Dedication

**This book is dedicated to
all you do-it-yourselfers in the world.**

May your saws
always cut straight,

May your drill bits
always be sharp.

May your next project require
no ER visits,

May you always hit the nail
on the head.

May all your projects require
only one trip to the store,

And may you complete all your projects
successfully!

*~~ Pamela Frost*

# CONTENTS

Acknowledgments    **viii**

Introduction    **x**

## 1  How Hard Can It Be?

| | | |
|---|---|---|
| A Handywoman's Tale | Cathy C. Hall | 2 |
| Getting a Handle on Life | Ernie Witham | 6 |
| Fuzzy Logic | Caroleah Johnson | 10 |
| It Looked So Easy | Heidi Griminger Blanke | 15 |
| The Rise and Fall of Ms. Fixit | Risa Nye | 21 |
| Flood or Fame | Kathe Campbell | 25 |
| The True Meaning of DIY | Dianne J. Wilson | 29 |
| The Tile Files | Lucia Paul | 33 |

## 2  WTF?!

| | | |
|---|---|---|
| Fan-dango | Mike McHugh | 40 |
| Power Play | Debra Ayers Brown | 46 |
| Kill a Watt? | Sheila S. Hudson | 51 |
| Euro Shock | Arthur Bowler | 55 |
| Plier-Lamping 101 | Kathryn Cureton | 58 |
| A DIY GPS | David Martin | 62 |
| Jolt of Reality | Camille DeFer Thompson | 66 |

## 3  The Magic of Wallpaper and Paint

| | | |
|---|---|---|
| Lines and Lions | Laurel McHargue | 72 |
| Nice Try | Harriet Cooper | 78 |
| Screw This | MaryAnn Myers | 83 |
| Caribbean Blue | Pamela Frost | 88 |

| | | |
|---|---|---|
| Coming Unglued | Terri Duncan | 92 |
| When the Wife's Away | John Reas | 97 |
| The Perils of Paint | Mary Mendoza | 104 |
| Steamed | Lesley Morgan | 108 |

## 4 Go with the Flow

| | | |
|---|---|---|
| Where Real Men Hang Out | Ernie Witham | 114 |
| What Comes Around Goes Around | Pamela Frost | 118 |
| The Domino Effect | Banjo Bandolas | 124 |
| The Powderless Powder Room | David Martin | 131 |
| The Missing Gene | Meg Mardis | 136 |
| Finally Flush | Maureen Rogers | 140 |
| Deep Doo Doo | Terri Duncan | 143 |

## 5 Martha Stewart Doesn't Live Here

| | | |
|---|---|---|
| Reverse-Engineering | Monica Giglio | 150 |
| Peach Pits, Grits and Hissy Fits | Cappy Hall Rearick | 154 |
| Pinterest Made Me Do It | Abigail Green | 159 |
| Chase to the Cut | Lisa Tognola | 163 |
| An Uncontrollable Urge | Judi Tepe | 169 |
| Let's Get Crafty | Cindy Kloosterman | 172 |
| Anyone Can Do It | Tracy Winslow | 178 |

## 6 It Seemed Like a Good Idea . . .

| | | |
|---|---|---|
| Free Labor, Anyone? | Pat Wahler | 182 |
| Stick-to-itiveness | Beth Bartlett | 186 |
| Rooftop Free-fall | Dianna Graveman | 189 |
| The Formation of Death | Kari Collins | 192 |
| News of the Day | Linda O'Connell | 196 |
| It Hits the Fan | Pamela Frost | 200 |
| Burned Out | Suzanne Olsen | 204 |

## 7 Spare Parts

| | | |
|---|---|---|
| He's Not That Into Me | Stacey Gustafson | 210 |
| Awl in the Family | Mike McHugh | 214 |
| Monument to Manhood | Cindy Hval | 220 |
| In Hot Water | Gloria Hander Lyons | 224 |
| Project Man | Maggie Lamond Simone | 227 |
| In Pursuit of Perfection | Timothy Martin | 230 |

## 8 Better Lawns and Gardens

| | | |
|---|---|---|
| Rock of Ages | John Schlimm | 236 |
| Thou Shalt Not | Shari Courter | 241 |
| A Zillion Zinnias | Terri Elders | 245 |
| Muddy Waters | Stephanie Fellenstein | 250 |
| He Who Kills Weeds | Stacey Gustafson | 254 |
| It Had to Be Yew | Lesley Morgan | 258 |
| Teamwork | Alice Muschany | 263 |
| Letting Go | Tori Nichols | 267 |

## 9 Women Who Get'r Done

| | | |
|---|---|---|
| I Can Do Anything | Bobby Barbara Smith | 272 |
| Bait Me | Pat Nelson | 278 |
| The Mystery Machine | Jill Pertler | 282 |
| Up Against a Brick Wall | Suzanne Olsen | 285 |
| GDCS | Susan Swartwout | 292 |
| Even if Askew | Janet Sheppard Kelleher | 296 |
| It's All Good | Sally Fingerett | 299 |

| | |
|---|---|
| **NYMB Series Founders** | **308** |
| **NYMB Co-Creator** | **310** |
| **Contributor Bios** | **312** |
| **Story Permissions** | **320** |

# Acknowledgments

You are all the greatest!

**From Pamela:**

Thank you to my guardian angel for helping me survive all my home improvement projects. She's been a busy little angel and deserves a day off.

Thank you to all the others who have helped me grow as a writer. For fear of leaving some important person off the list, I'll just say thank you to all the people who believed in me. I also want to thank all the people who didn't, because they made me stronger.

And thank you to my son, Chris Kmit. I'm sorry for making you hate home improvement.

**From Dahlynn and Ken:**

Thank you to Dahlynn's teen son Shawn. Another book is done and life at home may return to normal, "may" being the operative word. There are five new books in the pipeline!

Thank you to Shayla Seay for her kick-ass help in the office. Her ability to keep us organized is so amazing and her can-do attitude makes our crazy work life much easier.

And thank you to Pat Nelson for her excellent proofing skills. This means the world to us because her grandkids were visiting for a week when we sent her the manuscript. Pat told us she read between fun outings and when the kids were plugged in to their video games. You are an awesome proofer, friend, grandma and juggler!

**And from all of us at Publishing Syndicate:**

A special thanks to the many writers who submitted stories for this book. Without you, this book would not have come together like it did. Your stories were wonderful and we thank you for sharing them with us and the world. We only wish we could have printed every story submitted. Please keep those stories coming in for future NYMB titles: www.PublishingSyndicate.com.

# Introduction

*A man's got to know his limitations.*

~~ Clint Eastwood as Dirty Harry
in *Magnum Force* (1973)

Knowing your limitations can make life so much easier, but do-it-yourselfers often miscalculate when it comes to home improvement.

Human beings are not born do-it-yourselfers. We come into this world quite helpless. But it doesn't take long before a toddler pushes away his or her parents and utters, "I can do it myself." Some parents weep.

Home improvement projects often bring a person to tears, too, but with the passage of time, the tears turn to laughter. Luckily, the ability to laugh precedes the drive to do-it-yourself.

So is it nature or nurture? That's a tricky question.

One might say I was a born do-it-yourselfer. I come from a long line of people who just seem to know how to fix things. My grandfather was something of a DIY legend in his rural community in West Virginia. The DIY gene passed down from him to me. Friends have often called me "Mrs. MacGyver" or, in reference to one of my favorite TV personalities—Norm Abram of *This Old House*—"Lady Norm." I'm not bragging, just stating a fact. I can fix just about anything. Except people. I gave up trying and life is much happier.

While some people do seem to be born with a certain

amount of natural DIY talent, others are doomed to pick up the phone every time something needs repairing and maybe they are the lucky ones. What is most interesting to me is that despite the fact that do-it-yourself projects often don't go well, we continue to attempt them, over and over again.

Sometimes the urge to try any home improvement project catches a person by surprise. After all, when you first step through the portal of your local home improvement store, you know you're venturing into do-it-yourself purgatory. But there's no feeling in the world quite like standing back and admiring a DIY job well done. Except the look of marvel on your friends' and family's faces when you tell them you did it yourself.

I will close with the do-it-yourselfers' motto "How hard could it be?" Dirty Harry knows. Do you?

~~ *Pamela Frost*

# CHAPTER ONE

# How Hard Can It Be?

---

Famous last words . . .

---

# A Handywoman's Tale

by
## Cathy C. Hall

When my nephew fell into one of my closet doors, accidently knocking it off its track, I wasn't too concerned. I fancy myself quite the handywoman. I was sure it was just a matter of a *bang, bang* here and a *tap, tap* there and all would be right with the world once again.

To the room I went with my handywoman tools, ready to fix that pesky closet door. No matter how much I banged or tapped, I couldn't get it back into its track. So I pulled it completely off to get a better look.

The closet door was pretty darn heavy, but once I crawled out from under it, I could see a plastic piece had broken on the bottom of the door. Apparently, it's a rather important plastic piece, since it allows the door to slide in its track.

*Piece of cake*, I thought, as I headed to my local Home Depot store to find my helpful guy. I could have happily spent half a day looking for the elusive piece myself, but I always find a guy. It's a bonding thing.

"I need this plastic piece," I said cheerily.

He took the piece from my hand and scrutinized it carefully. "This plastic piece?" he asked.

Regular people might be annoyed by this sort of questioning, but not us handywomen. It's all part of the bonding experience. "Yep," I said, "this piece right here. It's from a closet door."

"Huh."

I never like to hear that "huh." It's Step One in the "we-have-a-problem" experience.

"You can't buy that piece," he said.

See what I mean. It was a problem.

"Can I get another piece of something that would work?" I asked. That's a trick we handy types use.

"Hmmm."

Uh-oh. We had just moved to Step Two in the Problem.

"I think you're going to have to buy a new door," he said, pointing me in the direction where all the new doors patiently waited for new owners.

*OK,* I thought, once I found my way to the new door aisle, *I don't need an entire door, but I do need a little plastic piece. And this one is just $30.* So I loaded up the inexpensive door and took it home.

That evening, my 15-year-old son and his friend happened to be hanging out in the room that happened to be missing the closet door. The new closet door was pretty darn heavy, so I asked these fine young fellows to handle the situation. I left them with the plastic piece, the new door and easy-to-follow instructions.

"Mom!" my son called downstairs after 10 minutes. "This isn't working."

*Isn't that just like a male?* I said to myself. I trudged upstairs to take control of the situation.

Together, the three of us heaved and pushed. We grunted and we groaned. But we could not get the new door to stay in its track. Finally, we lowered the door to the ground to get a different view of things. What I noticed right off the bat was a missing plastic piece, the very same plastic piece that sent me on my quest in the first place.

"Where's the little plastic piece?" I asked. Thinking back, I might have said it loud enough for the neighbors to hear.

"You said to hammer it into that hole," answered my son, his face suddenly gone sheet white.

"So we d-did," stammered his friend

Upon closer inspection, I determined that the boys had hammered the little plastic piece really deep into its little home. Not even the tip of the small part was visible. So there I was again with a perfectly good closet door that wouldn't stay in its track. At this point, both fine young men made tracks out of the house.

I stacked the new door in the garage with the old door. Yes, I could have returned the new door, but then I would have had some explaining to do. And I have a reputation to uphold among the handywomen at Home Depot. One fiasco like this can undermine years of bonding.

So I bought another door.

This time, I took care of business myself. I carefully pounded the little plastic piece into its little home. I hefted the door into the top track where it clicked into place. Ah, it was music to my ears. Now all I had left to do was tackle the bottom track with its little plastic piece.

My arms ached. My back muscles cramped. Back and forth, up and down went the door. But it would not settle into its track. "Argh!" I moaned. Then I had an epiphany: *Why not just settle the door from the bottom side first?* I chuckled out loud at my own foolishness. We handywomen are allowed to do that.

I lowered the door into its track. It promptly fell out. I lowered it again. It fell out again. Remember that little plastic piece? I realized it wasn't the correct size, so it didn't fit properly into the track.

I returned to Home Depot for a THIRD time and found another helpful guy. "Well, there's your problem," he said after hearing my story and asking the age of my house.

*Don't say it, don't say it, don't say it,* I prayed. *Don't say the words that make handypeople—men or women—shudder in their steel-toed shoes.*

"Lady, they just don't make that part anymore."

He'd said it.

I stacked the closet door in the garage with the other two closet doors. But since the chic designer look of a closet with only one door wasn't exactly working for me, I pulled the other door off its track. Then I hung some lovely curtains in front of the closet.

Now there are three closet doors stacked neatly in my garage. What, you ask, happened to door number four? It's currently resting across two filing cabinets in my office, turning the door into a fine, extra-long desk. I must say, we make a great team, my closet door and me.

Didn't I tell you I was quite the handywoman?

# Getting a Handle on Life

by
Ernie Witham

You can always tell a house with kids—the driveway is full of bicycles and skateboard ramps and the front door is standing open. I'm not sure what it is kids have against closing doors, probably something subliminal they've learned watching 15 hours of MTV every day.

I walked into our house holding the cat, which I had found stuffed inside a pair of Rollerblades. The cat was wearing a tiny pair of goggles and had a severely frightened look on its face. I automatically shut the front door. That's when I noticed the door handle on the floor, surrounded by various springs, clips and screws.

"Oh, man," I heard my teenager say from under a pile of soda cans and taco chip bags. "You didn't like close it all the way, did you?"

"What happened to the door handle?"

"I dunno. I tried to open it and it like exploded in my hand."

"Did you try turning it first, like I suggested?"

"Huh?"

I sighed. It was probably time for a new door handle anyway. The buildup of dried salsa made it hard to get your hand around the knob.

I headed off to the "we-have-everything" store. They had two door-handle/deadbolt combinations that looked similar to mine. One of them had been repackaged, as if someone had tried installing it, but it didn't fit. I bought the other one.

The great thing about people who write instructions for a living is that they always have a little surprise for you—usually hidden in the last paragraph. That's where I found the sentence that read: "Before drilling holes in your door, check the length of your backset."

The backset, which is part of the latching piece, is either 2-3/8 inches or 2-3/4 inches. My door, of course, already had holes. And guess what? Surprise! Surprise! My new, now almost completely installed door handle had the wrong backset.

I disassembled the thing and forced all the pieces back into the package exactly like the other one I had seen at the store.

The day was now more than half gone. Thus, it was time for "phase two" of home repair—the specialty hardware store. Here you'll find an amazing collection of clasps, hinges, locks and other homeowners, holding cardboard boxes full of exploded door parts. The salesman looked in my box and said, "Hmmm."

I've heard this before. It's not a good thing. That's when

I noticed the empty display space where front door handles used to be.

"Phasing these old ones out," he said. "And this woman needs one, too."

We sized each other up. Quickly, she pointed at the one right in front of me.

The salesman turned the display around. "Oops. Missing the lock cover."

I pointed at one a few feet away.

"Nope. Wrong size."

We both pointed at one in the corner.

"That's made for a door with two separate holes," the salesman said.

"I have two separate holes," we said in unison.

"Are they the same size?" the salesman asked.

I pointed at her shoe. When she looked down, I whipped out my cellphone and instantly dialed home. My nemesis tried to match my dexterity, but apparently she got a busy signal.

"Yup," my son said, after a few minutes. "I can stuff exactly the same number of Wheat Thins through both holes."

I didn't ask why he'd used Wheat Thins instead of a tape measure. I just winked at Miss Doorhandleless and told the salesman I'd take it.

"What size backset you got?" he asked.

"Two and three-quarters," I shot back, with confidence.

"Hmmm." There it was again. "This one's set up for 2-3/8ths. Guess I could change it."

"I have 2-3/8ths," the woman said.

"She's guessing!"

"Am not."

"Are too."

"Tell you what," said the salesman. "I have one in burnished gold and one in pewter."

"Burnished gold," we said in unison.

Another guy wandered into the door-handle section, carrying a cardboard box. He waved at the salesman.

"OK," I said. "I'll take the pewter."

It was nearly five o'clock by the time I finished installing the new door handle. I took a few minutes to admire my efforts, turning the handle, locking the lock, listening to my backset back setting. Then I went into the bathroom to wash my hands. The minute I closed the door, I heard a voice.

"Dude, whatever you do, don't flush."

# Fuzzy Logic

by
Caroleah Johnson

It's good to know your limitations in life. There are not many DIY projects I won't tackle unless, of course, it involves running heavy equipment or fixing car engines. Those things are completely out of my realm of know-how and beyond my desire to obtain such knowledge. But I've pounded nails, taken up flooring and painted ceilings in between sewing prom dresses, creating newsletters and fixing gourmet meals.

I wouldn't say that I have a wealth of expertise as much as simply an exaggerated sense of can-do-it-ness. It probably stems from the when-there's-a-will-there's-a-way message I received so often growing up. That mindset, though, has created a number of interesting, if not hilarious, predicaments, like the day I decided to do something nice for my husband.

I was starting menopause and still having a hard time admitting I might not be capable of doing all the things I used to do, thanks to aching joints, a bladder that no longer held great quantities of liquids and a few extra pounds. Plus, I had a severe case of what I call "fuzzy logic"—that lapse between what the brain thinks is possible and what the body is able to do.

But I didn't let those things deter me from my plan to surprise my husband. The garage was going to be reroofed Saturday, so I decided to tear the old roof off myself the day before to save my husband from the chore when he got home from work. We'd been married long enough for me to be past baking brownies to express my love. No, we were at the stage of true grit—the stage where love is expressed in actions, not flowery prose and sexy lingerie (although I have nothing against either of those). I reasoned that what my husband would appreciate most would be physical labor.

The idea came to me the previous evening when I spotted an odd-looking rake in the garage. "What's that thing?" I asked my husband.

"That's a rake for taking the old shingles off the roof."

"Oh."

And so began the plotting. Nothing more was said about the roof that evening and I tried to act as nonchalant as possible. I schemed to myself. I didn't have to work Friday and my overinflated sense of can-do-it-ness never considered the possibility that I was not as fit as I had once been. This is where my fuzzy logic took over: *How hard could it be to take shingles off a roof? A couple of hours and it'll be done.*

As soon as my husband left for work Friday morning, I slipped into my old Levi's, slathered on sunscreen and donned a sunhat, as well as a pair of leather gloves. I started out the door then remembered I should also take a bottle of water and my cellphone, just in case. I never thought to see how much battery life the phone had left. I was on a mission of love and nothing was going to stand in my way.

Upon retrieving the shingle rake from the garage, I looked for a ladder, but all I could find was a rickety old stepladder that had weathered too many seasons unprotected from the elements. I studied it for a few moments. *It doesn't quite reach all the way to the eaves*, I reasoned to myself. *Oh well, it will have to do.*

Still determined to do this nice deed, I set the stepladder near the back of the garage and started my ascent. Standing on the top rung, I had to hoist myself onto the roof with considerable effort. I knew I would have to stay on the roof until I was finished because I wasn't going to try tackling that ascent again. *Better leave the water alone.*

I attacked the shingles with all the gusto of my youth—for about an hour. Then my efforts slowed considerably. This was backbreaking work, but I was determined to finish the job. Even catching the seat of my pants on a nail and ripping a large hole in them didn't stop me. There weren't any neighbors close by, so I plodded away in my open-air britches. Between hot flashes and the warmth of the sun, my resolve to leave the water alone evaporated quickly in the rising heat. *Surely my bladder could hold for a couple of hours.*

Four hours later, when I pulled the last shingle loose, I was ready to collapse. I was also in dire need of emptying my bladder since I had consumed the entire contents of my water bottle. I gathered my things and inched toward the ladder. Once down, my plan was to wash up, comb my hair and look like I had been a lady of leisure all day.

The one thing I hadn't considered was getting back on that rickety stepladder. I stretched my legs down over the edge of the roof, but they barely touched the top step. To make matters even worse, the stepladder wobbled with the slightest touch. *Damn!* I sat on the edge of the roof in a small state of panic. I have a fear of heights that I worked hard to suppress while working on the roof. Now, looking over the edge, it was insuppressible.

I hated to do it, but I decided to call someone to help me get down. I pulled the phone from my pocket and stared at a blank screen. No display. Nada. Completely dead. I looked at the pile of discarded roofing and nails on the ground, and then the tipsy stepladder. If the stepladder fell with me on it, I was going to have more than just a hole in my pants. But how in the world was I going to call 911 with a dead phone? *Maybe I'll stay up here until my husband comes home.*

I might have stayed right there on the roof except for that blasted water. My bladder wasn't going to hold it much longer. I looked at the sun, trying to determine what time it was and how long before my husband would be home. I weighed my options—take a chance on the stepladder or try to explain to my husband why there was a big wet spot on the plywood. I knew the latter option would be a source of teasing for a very long time. I decided to keep that alternative as my absolute last resort.

For the better part of the next hour, I intermittently prayed and engaged in self-talk. *You got up here, you certainly can get down. You're not a wuss. How bad can it be? Just do it.*

The power of positive affirmation was not working, but the call of nature was starting to scream. I rolled onto my stomach and inched backward off the roof in the direction of the stepladder, simply hoping not to break any bones when it tumbled. Amazingly, it stayed upright. Once safely on the ground, I hustled into the house and to the bathroom, with no time to waste.

As the afternoon wore on, every muscle in my aching body reminded me that this may not have been one of my better ideas. After a hot shower and a couple of Tylenol, I returned the shingle rake to the exact spot my husband had left it and vowed not to say anything about my dilemma on the roof.

My husband was beyond surprised and delighted when he came home to find the roof ready for new shingles. "How did you get up there?" he asked. "All of the tall ladders are on my work truck."

I pointed to the old stepladder.

He looked at the stepladder then at me, with disbelief written all over his face. "That ladder? I'm surprised you didn't fall. I've been meaning to throw it away."

I didn't tell him that I was equally surprised. Sound logic would have made me think twice about ever climbing that stepladder. But a DIYer on a mission of love doesn't have to be logical, does she?

# It Looked So Easy

by
## Heidi Griminger Blanke

I've always dreamed big when viewing myself as a do-it-yourselfer. Even as a college student, long before the Internet, I culled pictures from magazines, copied instructions from books and planned for all the fabulous ways I could incorporate these ideas into my life. I still have the notebook, and I am still dreaming big. Perhaps, though, it's time to wake up.

Several years ago, during a day off from work, I decided to convert a coat closet into a pantry. How hard could that be? I'd watched it being done many times on HGTV and I even had books to guide me through the project.

The pantry was part of a back-door-entry makeover, inspired by home décor guru Christopher Lowell's television show *Interior Motives* and his principle of seven layers of design. At least that was my intention. I may have skipped a layer or six. The process involved nailing pieces of wood to the closet's side walls as shelf supports then placing the shelves on top of them. My plan was that if I started early in the morning, I would have a new and improved pantry ready for action by dinnertime.

I was distracted from the start. After emptying the closet of our coats and winter items, I surveyed the area for an alternate location. That's when I spied a 3-foot span of empty wall, lodged between the backdoor and the kitchen entry, begging for a coat rack. I could make a coat rack, too, as I was sure I must have seen Christopher do it at some point. I never missed Christopher's show, rearranging my work schedule around his genius.

I measured the wall, calculated the number of hooks I could install and added the supplies to my shopping list. It would look so pretty, and wouldn't take much doing, just a length of scrap wood topped by a wonderful piece of molding, both painted a glossy white and outfitted with five large brass hooks. Christopher used moldings all the time. Below that I would place a bench, culled from the garage and topped with a cushion in room-coordinated fabric. Christopher used loads of fabric and sewed everything right on the air in no time at all. I added black paint to my list (didn't I hear somewhere that every room should have something black?) and guesstimated the amount of fabric, piping and foam for the cushion.

The list grew. I went to Home Depot and asked for a 1x2 for the shelf supports.

"What kind do you want?" the salesperson asked.

"One-by-two," I replied.

"But what kind of 1x2?" he insisted.

"They come in kinds?"

The salesperson patiently explained the intricacies of choosing a 1x2.

"And," I continued, "I need wood for the shelves."

"What kind of wood?"

I explained the project, bought the materials and a mitering box and saw, but decided to skip the coat rack for the time being. My ego wasn't ready to face a discussion on how to attach the molding to the scrap lumber. Plus, I secretly worried the salesperson would ask me what kind of molding.

By noon, I was ready to take on the world, or at least the closet. Christopher transformed his rooms without even changing into work clothes, though I had an apron nearby for painting. But first, I ate lunch. I needed some fuel for the job.

While not schooled in woodworking, I knew enough to measure twice and cut once, so I did. Eight pieces of wood were ready to be nailed as supports. I envisioned everything dropping into place, especially since I had planned ahead and purchased a label maker on eBay so that everyone in my family could return items to their designated places. Locating cleaning supplies, pet articles and small household items would no longer be part of a frustrating game of hide-and-seek. It felt so good to be so handy.

Because even I knew straight lines mattered in this kind of work, I marked the intended support placement lines with a level. It took me 10 minutes to do the first side, but 45 minutes to do the second side as I had to determine how to assure both sides measured the same distance from the floor. I didn't count the 25 minutes it took me to locate the yardstick.

I held the first support to the wall, grabbed a nail and

hammered it in. The nail bent before the tip could make it through the wood and into the wall. I tried another, with more success, but when I gave a tug to assure the support's stability, the damn thing pulled right out of the wall. I'd forgotten to nail into the studs. I quickly located them as an existing upper shelf had already been installed using this method. I followed suit in placing the nails, but they still bent as I hammered. Maybe Christopher used a nail gun. So instead, I turned to screws, only stripping three or four.

By mid-afternoon, the supports were in place and I set to work cutting the shelves. In retrospect, I should have had them cut at the store, but that would have meant bringing the measurements with me, which, of course, I did not do. The sawing was hard and frustrating work. I chided myself for not paying more attention to how Christopher cut wood, as my shelving lumber did not fit neatly, or at all, into the miter box. I cussed, I cried and I swore never to attempt another do-it-yourself project. After an hour of sawing, I had four shelves with jagged edges.

It was time to paint, but first I had a snack. No sense in ruining a good cup of coffee and a scone with paint fumes. My teenagers came home from school midway through the closet's first coat. "Who wants to help me paint?" I asked in my best enticing mom voice. Backpacks dropped, the refrigerator opened, bathroom doors closed and the kids asked what we were having for dinner.

I gritted my teeth and glared at their retreating backs. I opened the refrigerator and poured myself a giant glass of chocolate milk, went to the bathroom and waited for the first coat of paint to dry. I then smoothly applied the second coat. Christopher designates layer one of the seven layers of design as paint and architecture. With this part finished, I was well on my way.

My husband, Scott, arrived home and examined the project. He gently asked about the uneven shelf cuts, the paint on the floor and the pile of winter items blocking the path to the laundry area. However, he had never watched Christopher Lowell and knew less about do-it-yourself than I did. We are both offspring of urban parents who grew up in flats and apartments, not on farms. Do-it-yourself might have involved hanging a picture or tightening a screw somewhere. For everything else, we called in the experts. Our learning curve was a flat line.

Together, Scott and I lifted the first shelf onto its support. Like manna from heaven, it was a joy to behold. The jagged edges butted up against the wall, so they didn't show. The shelf fit smoothly and was level. Three more shelves to simply drop into place and perhaps we'd go out to dinner to celebrate my do-it-yourself success.

The second shelf fit, but snugly, requiring a bit of force to lock it into place. The third shelf was too long, settling in at an angle. I stared in disbelief, yelled at the shelf, and then grabbed a hammer to knock the stupid thing into submission. I channeled Cinderella's stepsisters, determined to force the shelf into its supports like a big foot into a tiny glass slipper.

Scott pried the hammer from my grasp.

He ordered a pizza for dinner and banned me from the room—from my own project. Then he spent the next hour trimming the last two shelves and finished my project for me.

I went off to sulk. Everything Christopher did worked the first time without a hitch. How the hell could I have been so misled?

Over the next few days, I filled the shelves, labeling baskets and boxes. It didn't look half bad. I made the coat rack and a bench cushion, both of which had a definite homemade essence about them.

Recently, I watched Christopher create a partial bed canopy, which would look great over the basement sleeper sofa, giving it a more finished look. I wondered what kind of wood I would need for that . . .

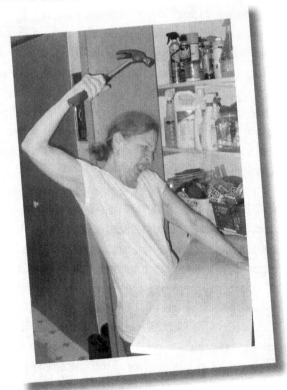

Heidi

# The Rise and Fall of Ms. Fixit

by
Risa Nye

"How hard could it be?" I asked.

"Those words will be engraved on your tombstone," my friend Chris replied, as we hoisted her new television into its cabinet.

I just didn't see why two able-bodied women had to wait until the man of the house arrived home to hook up her equipment. The two of us read the manual, followed directions, did a bit of heavy lifting and got the job done.

I have always been the one to figure out where the leak or squeak is coming from. I have fixed plumbing, replaced light fixtures and changed furnace filters, not to mention dealing with ailing appliances and putting furniture together. No pink tools for me, either. I am woman . . .

Therefore, I approached the replacement of a damaged part on my garage door with a great deal of confidence. My teenage daughter got a little too close to the door frame when she pulled the car out of the garage one morning, leaving a large dent in a section of the trough-like metal track that guides the wheels of the door as it rises.

To replace the part, I ventured out of the city into the industrial no-man's land where the garage-door-opener parts place squatted among all the other boxy buildings. I had removed the section of dented metal track and brought it with me, so there could be no mistake about what I needed to buy. I received a few skeptical looks from the guys behind the counter, but I'm used to it. I have purchased ball cocks at the plumbing supply place and I am cool with that. I am Ms. Fixit.

Once I got home with the replacement piece, I figured I would push the red button that started the door on its upward journey, just to see what would happen. True, there was a piece of the track missing, but was I concerned with that? No, I was not.

As the door rose, its mounted wheels rolled up the track, like the ones on those expensive wooden toy trains from Sweden. At that moment, I realized the missing piece of metal track, the one I had just bought and now held in my hand, served a very important function. Without it, the door began swaying slightly, which started a Rube Goldberg-like series of events resulting in the wheels popping out of the track one at a time. I stood mouth agape, watching the train wreck. In this case, the caboose was my garage door.

After a few heart-stopping moments, the door had popped all its wheels and hung, hammock-like, from the garage ceiling by two strands of twisted cable wire as thin as spaghetti. I started to shake. Could the door fall down? My garage had two stories above it. Would the whole thing collapse like a house of cards? And what was I thinking when I took on this project? "How hard could it be?" I recall myself saying.

The real question is—*Was I thinking?*

I ran upstairs and grabbed the phone. With trembling fingers, I punched in the number of the place that had installed the garage door. I begged them to come, NOW!

"Well," the guy drawled, "it's almost 5:30. What with traffic and all, that's going to be time-and-a-half."

"Whatever, not a problem—just get here quick, please." I then went back downstairs to the garage to keep an eye on the swaying door.

Soon after I started standing guard, my son came home from school. His jaw dropped when he saw the sagging door and me pacing like a maniac in front of it. He stood there watching me, and I knew he wanted an explanation. But instead, I barked an order. "Just go inside . . . GO!" He went.

Meanwhile, a couple of my neighbors drove by, waved and pointed at our new "Sway-backed Garage Door of Doom."

"Something wrong?!" they shouted when they saw my predicament.

"No, no, nothing. All under control." I waved them on.

Time crept by. The other two kids came home. I was now a roiling ball of self-hatred and anxiety.

Finally, the garage door repairman arrived. He was a titan with muscular arms, long curly black hair and a neat goatee. I asked him, "Is this the stupidest thing you've ever seen?" And without waiting for his answer, I added, "Can you fix this?"

"I can fix it," he said.

And he did. He lifted the door, Atlas-like, with his bare hands.

His grease-covered fingertips made a dainty border up the sides of the white garage door as he put the wheels back on the track and secured the new piece of metal to the door frame.

He pushed the red button; the door went up and down. Perfectly.

I paid him. He left.

His fingerprints are still there, though, a reminder that some things are harder than they look.

Risa, her garage door and the repairman's fingerprints

# Flood or Fame

by
## Kathe Campbell

"Where does it say in the plumber's manual that the wife sweats the pipes?" I said, arguing mercilessly with my husband, Ken.

"I can't believe you're backing down on this one, Kath. Sweating pipes is something all women should know how to do. Right, girls?" Our two young daughters sensed the onset of a clash and raced upstairs, while I murmured a small "Shit!" out of earshot.

We were building our dream house, which I had designed and drafted. It was up and enclosed. Heat ducts, PVC drains, electrical and most appliances were in place. There had been no surprises, except one awful realization that the rec room entry to the basement had been cemented solid after somebody neglected to frame a doorway. I stood thunderstruck, wondering if tearing down a piece of wall would be next on Ken's list of duties. My heavy-duty job prayers must have worked, for

Ken dutifully donned protective glasses and a mask, picked up the jackhammer and eventually broke through amid clouds of dust.

We had all the comforts of home—except water. It did no good pleading a plumbing reprieve. As Ken trotted out the propane torch, solder, paste, flux, sandpaper and the ladder, he protested, "We can't finish putting up Sheetrock and trim until the plumbing is in place, dear. I need your artistic touch."

Artistic touch indeed. What a con man. I resented being bamboozled into mastering a trade for a union I didn't belong to.

Nonetheless, after considerable thought, I resolved to inspire the female side of our tribe by displaying feminine grit and genius. *What can be so hard*, I pondered while staring at lengths of copper pipe, elbows, T's, sleeves and the hacksaw? It most likely entails measuring, cutting and fitting the pieces together with some Stickum then waiting for it all to dry.

Wrong!

Admiring my husband's eternal know-how in all things, I bravely buckled under, on one condition: "No yelling if this place leaks like a sieve when I'm finished."

It was a deal.

My heart finally retreated from my throat and a new feeling of confidence replaced the shrinking violets in my tummy as Ken demonstrated the process. I figured it didn't look so terribly hard. Since Ken knew the exact placement of the pipes, he agreed to measure and cut while I prepped.

With each span strapped to beams and framing, we moonlighted our nights away like a couple of pros. Ken polished pipe ends then I slathered them with flux, inserted needed sleeves and torched and soldered until they ran red-hot. Our shining copper stretched out into a jungle of twists and turns like a giant labyrinth beneath the kitchen and bathrooms, forming mini-mazes all the way to the basement. Catching an occasional 2x4 on fire, I quickly snuffed it out while thoughts of a hot shower and a flushing toilet made me delirious.

Finally, we were done. The magic moment had come. We all crossed our fingers and said a prayer as Ken rushed downstairs to the main turn-on. The kids and I then made tracks to our appointed stations, impatiently lying in wait for Mother Nature's first precious trickles originating from Montana's Big Hole River. The house was deathly still, nearly overwhelming me with tingles coursing up my spine while waiting beneath the kitchen sink for flood or fame. The sound of water coursing through virgin copper sounded heavenly until finally, only a small gurgle, and then nothing. Oh, that blessed nothing, the sweetest moment of silence on earth.

We hugged and danced around atop bare floors until our new digs shook. Raising paper cups in toast, my husband put his arm around my shoulder and announced he would hang the last of the Sheetrock and we could move in, "Just as soon as your mother hooks up all the sink and toilet fittings."

As I proudly crouched beneath the cold and dispassionate

porcelain receptacles, I fancied my entry into the Plumber's and Pipefitter's Union, with my artistic touch, of course.

Have torch—will travel!

Kathe

# The True Meaning of DIY

by

## Dianne J. Wilson

Like most countries, South Africa can be neatly split up into the super-rich who have it all and the dirt-poor who face daily challenges.

"My family and I," you ask? We're stranded somewhere in the murky land in between. We don't go hungry, but we seldom have wads of spare cash to throw at home improvement. When we do get that rare extra bit, spending it on a contractor to do a project we could do ourselves seems nothing short of stupid.

Our house started its life as a modest two-bedroom affair, with no garage, no built-in cupboards and no curtain rails. The bathroom was so small that if you sat down on the loo too quickly, you bumped your head on the opposite wall. The house's original tiling had been kept to a minimum—there were just two rows around the tub and the same around the kitchen sink. And every inside wall was painted pink. Pink.

The day we moved into our little goldfish bowl was rather bizarre. Since we had no cupboards, we had nothing to unpack things into. And with no curtain rails, there was nothing to hang window coverings on. So we settled for making beds and arranging furniture and boxes. My mom saved the day and our modesty when she went out for lunch and came back with curtain rails.

Over the years, our motley collection of cupboards, children and assorted bits of furniture grew to the point that you couldn't turn around too quickly in any room without sending something crashing. The lawnmower had taken up permanent residence under the kitchen table, and the weed eater lived behind the couch with the garden umbrella. Like I said, we had no garage.

Don't get me wrong, we had made some improvements. The pink walls had died along the way, replaced with soothing shades of white and blue. My two-year-old's choice was yellow. The tile in the bathroom and kitchen had grown to cover entire walls. A lawn and something resembling flower beds had replaced the wall-to-wall weeds that had been our garden. And we were happy. Granted, we weren't very organized, but we were happy.

Crisis hit when I had to start working from home. Somewhere in this melee, we needed to come up with a functioning office for an efficient mom/business person. It was time for Phase 2—two new bedrooms, one with an en suite bathroom. Heaven! So armed with a borrowed cement mixer, some books and blissful ignorance, we decided to become do-it-yourselfers.

We paid the price. I'm talking about shovel blisters from digging foundations and screaming back muscles from carting wheelbarrow loads of bricks closer to the building site. Heck, I'd even memorized the recipe for perfect foundation cement. My greatest fear during this whole process was that the cement dust from the mixer would chemically react with the mucus in my nose and I'd never breathe through my nostrils again. Home improvement can be scary stuff.

At one point, to my hubby's dismay and my utter delight, we admitted defeat and called in the troops to get the house back to a livable state. My scathing view of the stupidity of spending money to get help flip-flopped overnight. Egged on by the swelling of every new blister and the sweat-caked cement dust all over my body, I realized there are some things that a girl shouldn't do.

That's where we are today. We still have no garage and only a few cupboards, but now we definitely have more space to pile stuff. Our boxes have moved into the en suite bathroom until the budget stretches far enough to allow us to install a toilet, bathtub and basin. We're the only family I know with an en suite garage.

I've learned a lot through this process, much more than just the recipe for perfect cement. In fact, I've discovered the true, well-hidden meaning of DIY. Contrary to most misguided assumptions, DIY does not stand for "do-it-yourself." Speaking from much personal experience, a do-it-yourselfer is a "Drastically Insane Yobbo." My hubby's version would probably be more along the lines of "Divinely Inspired You."

You don't believe me? Give it a bash and decide for yourself.

Dianne

# The Tile Files

by
### Lucia Paul

It started with a modest dream. I wanted to replace the black and lime-green tiles in our master bathroom.

I know, I know. At this very minute, most women are drooling for a black and lime-green tile bathroom. What woman wouldn't want to apply her makeup in the flattering glow that only antifreeze-colored tile can deliver? Frankly, the aging process sped along every time I looked in the mirror because of this. Not to mention the fact that we spent a lot of unnecessary time in the ER thinking we were suffering from liver failure.

But I digress. I'd watched enough HGTV to know that someday we would want to sell this house and before doing so, we would need a more neutral and modern look in the master bath. I should mention that my husband watches home improvement like it's a sport. "C'mon! You call that a Sheetrocking?" Or, "You idiots! Tape it first! Tape it first!"

So the intersection of my design ideas and his competitive drive in home projects made the perfect combo to get this party started. And by party, I mean a trip to the tile store. And by tile store, I actually mean a tile store.

Some people get nervous walking into hospitals, others aren't fans of entering federal courthouses. I become a sweaty mess when I go into a tile shop. It can all be traced to a visit circa 1993 when I was picking out marble. Suffice it to say that by the time I left, not only was it clear that I knew nothing about marble, but also that the salespeople in the store felt that I was not qualified to even own marble and never would be.

It still smarts.

But this outing was a breeze. We decided on a theme of warm caramel for main tiles with a darker brown and cream accent tile. The salesman even seemed to think I was a pretty good tile-picker. So with my dignity intact, and about $1,500 worth of tile, we left the store.

"The demolition will be a cinch and you can help me," my husband stated confidently. My blood froze. I'd heard those words before. Only the scene in *Silence of the Lambs* where the scary guy says to his captive, "It puts the lotion on its skin" can make me more terrified.

Frankly, it—namely, I—would rather put the lotion on her skin than help with a demolition. This wasn't my first rodeo, as they say. I had helped with what will forever be known as "The Garage Demo of 2006." If your idea of a good time is dodging flying wood, nails and unknown fungal growths from a garage built at the turn of the 20th century, this project was for you. I favor home projects like folding laundry or wiping down the coffee table. I can't pretend my husband doesn't know what he's doing around the house, because he does. It's just his forge-ahead-at-all-costs style that can be challenging.

We decided to devote a weekend to the demolition, knowing that prying off 100-year-old tile would be tedious work. We're all about safety around here. I find that if I am about eight miles away from any home project, I can assure my well-being. But it's hard to actually assist if I'm not in the room.

Saturday morning, the day of the demolition, my husband announced he couldn't find his usual stash of ventilation masks, gloves and eye protection. He looked at me suspiciously.

I had been on an organizing kick, which translated means that I shoved all life's odds and ends into plastic tubs and stacked them in the basement. Thus, I had to find what he was missing. I made a half-hearted attempt to go through the tubs, and the bad news was that I didn't find any of those items, but I did find some baby photos. I spent a few happy minutes going through the photos until he yelled downstairs for me to hurry up.

Necessity is the motherhood of invention, and my husband had given birth to a doozy. Since I couldn't locate the required safety items, he handed me my snowmobile helmet and gloves. His were already on, so when he talked, he sounded like Darth Vader and looked a bit like him, too. I could have sworn he said Luke was my father, or maybe I was Luke's father, but I'm not quite sure.

He started the demolition with a hammer and chisel without the knowledge of one important thing—really old tile is often made of glass. The sharp stuff. The stuff that, if you take a hammer and chisel to it, comes flying at you in deadly shards.

It didn't take long before we both realized that this kind of tile needs to be taken off differently. Our first real clue was when several daggers of glass decided to lodge securely in my husband's arm. Snowmobile gloves don't extend to the elbow, unless you are going to a Black Tie snowmobiling event. My husband is not a person who asks for directions or cries "uncle!" in the first 20 minutes of any home project, even if blood, shards of glass and a terrified wife in a helmet are part of the drama.

Maybe it's because we had been watching *Band of Brothers* that he was so comfortable with the flying shrapnel that was the tile. "Duck! Incoming!" he boomed as he merrily hacked away at the tile wall.

We admitted defeat about an hour into the project. I had privately admitted defeat about 11 seconds in. When my do-it-yourselfer husband actually formed the words, "Call someone to come and finish this," I knew we had a difficult renovation situation on our hands.

That Monday morning, I secured a recommendation for a tile guy who specialized in older homes.

"Tell him it's going to be a hell of a job," my husband said, as he left for work. "And call me and tell me how the hell he does it."

Now we were on the same page. I made sure the tile guy was aware of our dire situation. "It's going to be a pretty challenging demo job. Take all the time you need," I said breathlessly, as I considered offering him a snowmobile helmet.

He nodded sagely and got to work. I was able to call my husband about two hours later to tell him that the demolition was complete and no one had lost a limb or even any blood.

"He's done?" my husband asked incredulously. "How did he do it?"

"Well, he took a circular saw and cut the tile and Sheetrock off in big squares," I said gently. There was silence on the other end of the phone. I didn't have the heart to tell him that as I watched the tile guy efficiently and easily cut out and stack the wall in about six sections, he asked, "You didn't try to actually pry this off, did you? You can get cut pretty bad that way."

Oh, it hurt all right, but I had family pride to protect. "Oh, heavens no! Goodness, who would even try that?"

He looked at the pair of snowmobile gloves and the telltale helmet my husband had left in the shower. "I can always tell. Demolition is never as easy as you think it's going to be."

Tell me about it.

The new bathroom and
the demolition safety
equipment

# CHAPTER TWO

# WTF?!

You're in for a real shock!

# Fan-dango

by
## Mike McHugh

Normally, I don't do wires. That's because wires tend to have these things called "electrons" running through them. You can't see electrons. They're very small and wear camouflage, but still, they are dangerous. And electrons have a lot of energy, more than a toddler who has just polished off a Hershey bar the size of a full sheet of plywood.

Did you know that if electrons are unleashed due to a wiring mishap, they can fry your brain? As evidence, look at what happened to Ozzy Osbourne after a stagehand's mistake with his microphone cable. And you thought it was the result of certain psychoactive substances.

No, electrons are way more dangerous than psychoactive drugs. Being that I like my brain the way it is, warts and all, you can understand my anxiety about the ceiling fan project.

"That fan is really shaking," my wife casually said one

morning, looking upward from where we sat at the breakfast table. Casual statements such as these always trigger the spousal alarm that takes root in men's heads from the moment they say, "I do." Statements that refer to subjects such as her mother and credit card limits also fall into this category.

In this case, I sensed an impending project, and this set my mind to working. No project ever succeeds without a well-conceived plan. My plan typically involves trying to avoid doing the project altogether. Thinking quickly, I also gazed up at the fan, stroking my chin in a ponderous manner, as if I were a doctor of ceiling fans.

"Well," I said, "it's just wobbling slightly. I'm thinking it's due to an imbalance of dust accumulation on the left ventricle probate shaft. Nothing to worry about. It'll be fine after a good cleaning."

"It's shaking more than a belly dancer with the delirium tremors, and besides, I just dusted it," she shot back. "No, we need to replace it."

For the benefit of you single readers, "we" is never a plural pronoun in the marital dialect of English. It almost always means "you," except when used in certain conjugations, as in the sentence: "We really need more space in the bedroom closet." Even then it is still singular.

"OK then," I answered. "Let's think outside the box. A new ceiling fan may not be the only option here."

"What do you have in mind?"

"Maybe we can get a few Hawaiian girls to fan us with palm fronds instead."

But she wasn't having any of that. My original scheme having failed, it was time to go to the backup plan. For me, this usually involves calling a contractor. But, in a small town such as mine, I knew word would eventually get out to my buddies, and I could not let that happen. Among guys, hiring a contractor to do such a simple project is looked upon in the same way as having your wife tie your shoes for you in the morning. With no other way out, I resigned myself to the fact that I would be doing this myself.

The first step of the project was to pick out the new ceiling fan. I am particularly bad at the picking-out-things juncture, having held up many an express checkout line deciding between paper and plastic. And so, I took my wife along on the trip to Ceiling Fan City. It was a good thing, too. There, we found a vast selection of fans in all shapes and sizes, some as big as cruise ship propellers. I left her to decide while I went off to get a 5-gallon bucket of spackle, which, in my experience, always comes in handy for projects such as these.

Once the new ceiling fan was home, the next step was to find and read the instructions in my preferred language. I prefer French for its tonal quality, but I can't read a word of it, and so I default to English. It's especially important to thoroughly review the safety warnings that appear in pages two through 14 (out of 15). These the manufacturer thoughtfully provides for the benefit of the consumer, as well as for its lawyers, who understandably don't want to be dragged away from their power lunches to go into court and defend their mega-client against pesky consumer lawsuits.

Before starting any installation, I also like to check and make sure that all of the parts listed in the manual are included. Rarely have I found anything missing, but once in a while I do find a few extra screws or whatnots. These the manufacturer sometimes throws in to keep the consumer on his or her toes. If you do not check this, you will get to the end of the project, notice these additional parts and wonder where you messed up. From that day forward, you will live in fear that, some night at a dinner party, the fan might suddenly drop out of the ceiling onto your plate and fling pureed turnips all over your Aunt Ruthie's new dress. It doesn't matter that no one will likely notice it on the pattern. Believe me, you do not want this to weigh on your mind.

Next, it was time to isolate the power to the circuit. (Remember those electrons!) Unfortunately, my circuit panel has more breakers than the Superdome and none are labeled. I thus had to resort to trial and error. I eventually found the right breaker—in the process setting every digital clock in the house to blinking, activating the security system and interrupting my wife's game show right before they revealed which briefcase held the million dollars. And, for your information, even though I live in the area, I didn't do this project during last year's Super Bowl in New Orleans. Besides, my team was winning before the blackout.

The installation went surprisingly well. This only served to heighten my fear that I'd done something terribly wrong. I even had enough spackle left over to possibly get me through the next project. My trepidation was confirmed once I turned the power back on. The fan had two switches—one for the light and one for the fan itself. They both worked as intended with the old fan. However, with the replacement I somehow ended up having a single switch control for both the light and the fan. Darn, I knew I should have used more spackle.

I was sure that I'd wired the new fan exactly as the old one. It was a simple circuit. I'd seen more complicated wiring on a toaster. Perplexed, I took down the new fan and double-checked the connections against the color-coded sketch that I'd carefully drawn before disconnecting the old one. OK, maybe using invisible ink for the white wires was being a bit too anal. Still, I was certain I'd done it right!

To me, having both functions on a single switch wasn't the end of the world. I could just use the pull chain to control the fan. I could live with it, but I knew it would be a problem for my vertically challenged wife. I would have to build a scaffold to give her access. I knew she was not going to be happy when I gave her the status report, which I peppered with a few choice swear words in my preferred language. (For this, I like German for its guttural quality.)

She took the news surprisingly well. She didn't even suggest that I try once more to rewire the fan, probably out of fear that, if I cut the power again, she'd miss out on guessing the secret phrase after a contestant's vowel purchase.

To this day, we are living with the single-switch arrangement for our breakfast room fan. I chalk it up as a success. Now, I know some of you talented do-it-yourselfers might disagree. You know who you are—you whose patios look like the Hanging Gardens of Babylon. But you've got to give me at least one moral victory.

And hey, at least the fan doesn't wobble anymore.

Mike and the fan

# Power Play

by
### Debra Ayers Brown

"Hey, when are you getting home?" my husband, Allen, asked me. He had called me at work. "I thought I'd tackle the exhaust fan in the bathroom you've been complaining about."

The hair on the back of my neck prickled—and with good reason.

My husband had many talents, but handyman wasn't one of them. I'd married him because he was smart enough to hire people to take charge of things. Before our marriage, he took his clothes to the drycleaners, his shoes to be polished and he hired a cleaning lady to come in to take care of his condo—the one we now shared. I was OK with the arrangement.

So I was stunned when Allen fixed a wobbly dresser drawer in our bedroom. It worked fine if you overlooked the two pointy nails sticking out an inch in front of the drawer. There was no real chance of bodily harm unless you forgot they were there and impaled yourself. Daddy took care of it on a weekend visit without any fuss.

From then on, when Allen mentioned fixing something, I always encouraged him to put it on a list for Daddy. Then one day, Allen snapped, "We don't need your father to take care of every little thing! You have me now!"

So I'd kept my mouth shut until now. However, an exhaust fan was a different matter. It involved electricity, a motor and possible power tools to replace it. *What is he thinking?* I said to myself when I hung up the phone.

The air sizzled when I entered our condo. A light showed from the powder room. A tool kit and dirty hand towels spilled out from the bathroom. I could hear Allen talking to someone behind the closed door.

*Good,* I thought, relieved he wasn't attempting this repair alone. Though my dad was handy, the gene skipped me. So I was of no help.

"I'm home," I called out to him.

"Damn!" came from behind the door before Allen stuck his head out, holding an electric drill in one hand. I looked around him and saw no one, making me want to spit nails. I hadn't signed up for any improve-, repair- or maintain-your-home duties. Plus, electricity, shock, pain and possible singed hair and eyelashes could be involved in this do-it-yourself project.

My worst nightmare came true when he said, "I've been waiting for you to help." Thus, I entered the dungeon of doom and joined him.

Allen wiped sweat from his brow with one arm and waved the drill toward the ceiling with the other. The cord whipped around enough to create a breeze. If he kept it up, we wouldn't need a new fan. He climbed up the rickety ladder to remove the screws from the fan plate.

"Oh, you should probably shut the power off. We don't need to get electrocuted," he said and directed me to the breaker box.

So I followed his orders, still not happy about it. I stared at the rows of breakers. "We're dead," I muttered, expecting to be crispy and extra-charred at any moment.

I held my breath and flipped one, and all the lights went out.

"Try another one!" came his disembodied voice.

I tried the next one and heard the air conditioner shut down.

"Not that one, either!" he shouted. "You need to find the master breaker that shuts off everything."

I found the right one through trial and error. With one flip of the switch, complete darkness enveloped us. No sound was heard from anywhere.

"Uh," he said as I returned to the bathroom, "I guess we need power for the power drill."

My fears ratcheted up a few notches. I had no confidence in either of our abilities. We couldn't even figure out how to use the power drill to get the screws out of the old fan. Not a good sign.

But I tried to be supportive and appreciate the fact he was trying. I knew better than to mention Daddy. Instead, I grabbed a screwdriver and the instructions and read each step to him. Somehow, he removed the screws and the old fan cover. No problems if you discounted the chunk of Sheetrock splattered on the floor.

Allen unplugged and pulled out the old fan. Screws pinged against the tile floor below. White specks from the popcorn ceiling floated down and settled on the counter and sink. Dust and man-sweat permeated the air of the small space. But confidence seemed to flow through Allen's entire body as he proclaimed, "We got it!"

After two trips to Hinesville Builders Supply to get a replacement that fit the old housing, Allen popped the new one in. He rubbed his hands on his jeans and announced, "Done."

"I'm impressed," I said, relieved since we had guests coming over for dinner the next night. Someone would be sure to use the powder room during the evening.

And they did. Halfway through the night, my best friend Becky rose from the couch and moved toward the bathroom, only a few steps away.

"Check out my handiwork," Allen said to her before she closed the door. He began to tell her husband exactly what we'd done.

In the small quarters, we could hear the light click on. In this case, Becky clicked on the light and without warning, a jet-engine roar wailed from the bathroom. Becky shrieked and ran back out to the group, looking from me to Allen, who now wore the most dejected look I'd ever seen.

"Oops. Sorry. We must have bought a defective exhaust fan," I said to her. "Run upstairs to our bathroom."

Many months later, Allen and I were able to talk about our adventure into home improvement when it came to the exhaust fan installation. The fan's jet-engine like roar was so loud that we joked about living near the airport when bathroom "convenience" was a necessity.

But when we could, we avoided the powder room until Daddy visited. Allen didn't say a word. He went back to taking his clothes to the drycleaners and his shoes to be polished. I took care of the house. With our power tools packed away in the back of a closet, we made a silent pact to never mention do-it-yourself again.

# Kill a Watt?

by
## Sheila S. Hudson

The summer of my discontent began early, in May. But the season of ironing with a flashlight in my pocket is forever on-going.

It was not always this way. When we remodeled our entry-way, the *piece de résistance* was a sparkling new chandelier gracing the stairwell. Dainty spirals of light pirouetted across the white banister and highlighted our new Berber carpet. That giddy sense of pride in a DIY job-well-done quickly changed to chagrin when I realized I would have to dust each and every one of those shards of glass in that dang chandelier.

But that was only part of the problem. It wasn't until I foolishly tried to iron while watching television that I realized I was teetering on the tip of the proverbial kilowatt iceberg. When the steam iron erupted, my bedroom plunged into the abyss of a pitch-black night.

Groping my way into the hall, I located the emergency

flashlight. With limited sight, I tromped down two flights of stairs to the basement, flung open the breaker box and frantically began flipping switches. I was home alone at the time, which added to my irritation. Mumbling to myself, I trudged back up the two flights only to witness the lights blink and go out again. Luckily, I still carried the flashlight.

I called the electrician who did the wiring. His telephone was no longer in service. I phoned my husband and it went straight to voice mail.

Did I mention that the air conditioning was off, also? I worked up quite a sweat. The stair climbing and stress triggered a hot flash, the arch enemy of women in the over-50 crowd. Needless to say, I wasn't a very happy woman at this point. Who is, when dealing with both menopause and no electricity?!

Alas, on my third trip downstairs, the light went on—not in the bedroom, but in my head. *It's the new chandelier! All those bulbs use up too many watts!*

I began my investigation. When the lights blinked off again, the chandelier in question was not turned on. *Hmmm . . . I wasn't using the lights in the master bath or the hallway.* There was another fruitless trip to the basement then upstairs again to find the lights still not on. I stood in the foyer, fists clenched. My low mumbles turned into words I wouldn't want my grandsons to hear. Then my husband came through the front door and casually inquired, "What's the matter?"

After explaining the situation and my frustration, he calmly told me what the problem was. "You're using too many watts. Turn off the makeup mirror light, the vanity light and the bathroom light. Oh, and don't forget the nightlight," he instructed. Then he plopped into the recliner and grabbed the television remote.

I stood there, floored. There were so many things wanting to leap from my mouth at him and his smugness, but I decided it wasn't worth it. Doing as he suggested was only a temporary fix because the lights blinked off again. By this point, I—not the iron—was steamed. That's when I gave up on ironing. Instead, I returned to the basement to vent my frustrations on the treadmill.

The gods smiled on me until that weekend, when I recklessly began my vacuuming regime. The over-wattage dragon reared its ugly head once again. I coped, but just barely. This time, I traversed the three flights of stairs only twice to flip breakers.

Later in the fall on an especially rainy, miserable evening, I plugged in the heating pad and adjusted it on my aching lower back. I nestled into the bentwood rocker in our bedroom, grabbed a mystery I had been reading and was thankful for the chance to relax. As the book's plot thickened, my aches subsided—but so did the lights on that entire floor. Only then did I remember our little electrical issue.

Stumbling in the dark, I tripped over a pair of shoes, stubbed my toe and ran my shin into the footboard of our king-sized bed. Groping along the bed's frame, I reached for my trusty purple flashlight, which was my constant companion.

I have learned that whenever I dry my hair, plug in the curling iron, turn on the television, iron or even vacuum, it is prudent for me to carry my little purple friend. I take it to my study. It lies on the counter when I shower or put on my makeup. I have flashlights in the kitchen drawer, in the medicine cabinet, beside the front door and in the pantry. My purple companion—or one of its clones—accompanies me whenever the lights blink off, and together, we traipse downstairs to flip the breakers. I realize we should probably call an electrician, but sometimes going to the breaker box is the only exercise I get.

If you ever come for a visit, I promise to leave the light on for you, just like they do at Motel 6. But bring a flashlight, just in case.

Sheila en route to the basement . . . again!

# Euro Shock

by
Arthur Bowler

Funny thing about Europe: it is a nice place to live, but alas, a few things are missing, such as pancakes, baseball and free refills. Oh, and overhead lighting fixtures.

In many European countries, when you move into a new house or apartment, you often have to take your own overhead lights with you and install them yourself—or at least try to. I had just moved from Massachusetts to Switzerland and was setting up an apartment in Zurich with my Swiss fiancée. It was an interesting adventure.

Unfortunately, home repair was not part of the curriculum during my years as a graduate student at Harvard Divinity School. Swearing was indeed touched on, and yes, thou shalt not. However, I believe that tools and colorful expressions in times of shock or anger tend to go hand in hand. One day, my faith in this premise was confirmed.

Regrettably, we do not always listen as carefully as we

should when our parents dispense advice: "Brush." "Wear a helmet." "Turn off the electricity before fondling electrical wires." In most of Europe, voltage runs 220 to 240 volts, compared with North America, which is 110 to 120 volts, far lower than in most other places in the world. But this difference would prove to be shockingly significant.

Standing on the seat of a wooden chair, Swiss Army knife in hand, I stared at two wires dangling through a hole in the ceiling and prepared to skin a bit of extra plastic off them before attaching the light. Looking back, it's ridiculous that two adults would actually witness such a scene and never even think about the obvious hazard involved. It may have been that we were too much in love to think. It may also have been that those who dabble in home improvement occasionally suffer from similar, fleeting lapses of intelligence.

I do not remember anything about the next few seconds. One moment I was standing on the chair, applying the steel knife to the wires, and the next moment I was lying on my back on the wooden parquet floor, dazed and wondering how I got there. My fiancée stared down at me, wide-eyed, hands over her mouth.

"Mein Gott! Are you all right? You did fly to the floor!" she said in broken English.

"I think so," I mumbled, and then muttered something else that would not be suitable in the chapel of the divinity school at Harvard. I shook my head from side to side and seemed to be OK, until I glanced at the Swiss Army knife in my hand—a chunk of the blade had been burned away.

It was my first euro shock. Luckily, it was the first and only electrical variety, but others were to follow: language, table manners, driving, even answering the telephone. For all of you who are involved with home improvement, I offer advice from the reverend. Think first. And when times are shocking, try a prayer and a swear. And by the way, swearing in German is *wunderbar*.

# Plier-Lamping 101

by
Kathryn Cureton

When I told my hillbilly husband, Hick, our lamp could only be turned on and off with pliers, he grunted. I took that to mean, "I, too, know what it is like to have a lamp that won't turn on or off without pliers. I will remedy that situation for you as soon as humanly possible, for I love you, and above all else, wish for you to be happy and have a lamp that works." Or not.

Three days later, I was still plier-lamping. I called Hick while he was in town buying dog food. "Get a lamp while you're there."

Hick cannot be bullied. Nor can he be persuaded to throw away a 17-year-old lamp with a broken switch. "I'll get a new relay to fix that one," was his answer.

He's always doing that, spouting out names of electronic gewgaws—like the word "relay"—that I do not comprehend. He might as well be telling a dog how to read the instrument panel on a 747. To me, a relay is a team of four runners in tiny shorts with colorful, uncomfortable-looking shoes with little or no support. Surely one good lamp-repairman could fix my light faster than four mediocre lamp-repairmen passing a baton amongst themselves. But I suppose we'll never know, because Hick returned home with neither a relay nor a lamp.

In his defense, he said, "That lamp still works. All you need is pliers."

Perhaps I am too much like Rosie Perez who played the character Gloria in *White Men Can't Jump*, wanting my personal Billy Hoyle to connect with me by sharing and understanding the concept of plier-lampedness. That's a lofty goal from the man who gave me a crutch to prop open the back hatch of my SUV when the hydraulic door-raiser broke. The same man who purchased a Garmin to measure miles per hour in the $1,000 Dodge Caravan he bought, the one with no speedometer needle. I don't know why Hick refuses to listen to the voice of reason. My voice.

Take the beginnings of the lamp incident, for example. I found out it wouldn't turn off when I woke up in my recliner at 2 A.M. in front of the big-screen TV. The lamp's plastic turny-thingy spun around without clicking. No darkness ensued. The plastic turny-thingy had cracked and no longer gripped the metal stem it enclosed.

I couldn't leave a lamp on all night! An overhead light, sure, but not a lamp. I was certain it would burn the whole house down! The plug to this lamp was behind the couch, where our 11-year-old son slumbered. I didn't want to wake the boy and send him upstairs to bed, so I figured it would be much easier to go to Hick's basement workshop and find pliers. This was a mother's dilemma: I didn't want the lamp to catch fire and turn my boy into a crispy critter before dawn. Because that's when lamps combust—at night. Not in the daytime—that's crazy talk. Everyone knows that lamps don't spontaneously combust during the day!

Hick says that lamps do not catch fire, ever. But he said the same thing about cars. Then his $300 car burst into flames when our son was cranking the starter as Hick sprayed ether under the hood. This was a car Hick saw sitting in a yard, with $400 written on the windshield, and thought it would make a good car to drive to work. The shirtless teenage boy who answered Hick's knock on the trailer door blurted, "I'll take $300 for it!" I think Hick learned a lesson there, and thus his splurge a few years later of $1,000 for the speedometerless Caravan.

Meanwhile, back at the lamp, I was determined to turn it off, lest the house burn down. Pliers in hand, I couldn't grip the lamp switch with the tool until I removed the shade. I had to unscrew that metal, thimble-looking doodad that held the shade in place. It was then I realized the doodad was hot, considering it had the light bulb shining on it all the live-long night. I found myself in a Catch-22. Normally, I would turn off the lamp and let it cool down before liberating the doodad to take off the shade. But the reason I was removing the shade was to turn off the lamp. It was like that O. Henry story, where the wife sold her hair to buy her husband a watch fob, while he sold his watch to buy her hair combs.

So I tried removing the thimble doodad with the pliers, but that wouldn't work. That's when I decided to use an oven mitt. Heading to the kitchen to retrieve one, I found myself wondering at what point one can safely say, *I sure got my money's worth out of that lamp. Seventeen faithful years. It's time to retire this one to Hick's barn workshop.* That's where nonworking appliances go to collect dust until Hick needs to scavenge a part from their lifeless bodies to repair other 17-year-old, broken-down appliances.

The oven mitt treatment was successful. I removed the shade and turned the lamp off using the pliers. For a few days, I had a shadeless plier lamp. Then Hick spliced some kind of wheel-turning thumb switch onto the lamp cord so I could put the shade back on. I suspect he only did that to get his pliers back.

After several false starts resulting from our intricate ballet of nagging and foot-dragging, Hick had my lamp up and running normally again within its 17th year. Apparently, there is a limit to the number of times he can ignore a heavy sigh and the proclamation, "I'm going downstairs to thumb on my patched-together lamp again." Now my former plier lamp has a new three-way switch and a one-way bulb. The bulb is Hick's subtle statement that I am not the boss of him. Sure, I have to click through off-off-ON. But now, I can use my fingers instead of pliers.

Kathryn's lamp and its off-off-ON switch

# A DIY GPS

by
## David Martin

A GPS unit is a wonderful invention for motoring adventures. For directionally challenged drivers like me, it's a godsend. Punch in an address and a pleasant-sounding disembodied female voice gently, but firmly, guides you to your destination.

But I don't often need a GPS unit in my car since I seldom stray far from my home. Ninety-nine percent of my driving involves retracing long-familiar routes.

What I really need instead is a personalized Global Positioning System to help me with my non-driving adventures. Something, say, like an interactive handyman's GPS to guide me through this week's home repair undertaking.

"Good morning, Dave. Please enter your project."

"Dave, I see you have entered 'rewiring the bathroom.' If my electronic memory serves me correctly, your last electrical repair job ended with you in the ER and a $500 repair bill for a licensed electrician."

"Very well. I am not here to judge you, simply to guide you."

"Yes, Dave, that is the correct screwdriver you need to remove the faceplate. One small bit of advice: best to first turn off the breaker switch for the bathroom. The breaker is located in the panel box in the basement."

"You're welcome, Dave. That's why I'm here."

"Oooh, that's a nasty shock! Which breaker did you turn off? Ah, yes, the first one you saw. Perhaps you should head back to the panel box and check for the switch labeled 'bathroom.'"

"Yes, Dave, the bathroom lights are on the same circuit. You're right—it is pretty dark in here. Often homeowners will start their repair jobs before 8 P.M. so they will still be able to see what they're doing."

"No, I did not mean to be sarcastic. My voice is not programmed for sarcasm. If you wish to continue with the repair job after the sun sets, it is not for me to judge."

"Yes, a flashlight would be a good idea, Dave. Two or three would be even better. A portable floodlight would be best. No, again, I am not programmed for sarcasm."

"Very good, Dave. You have removed the faceplate with no major injuries. Now unscrew the top and bottom screws and remove the outlet."

"It would have been preferable to unwind the wires from the screws before pulling out the outlet. But that's OK. Just push the electrical box back into the wall and use a bit of Polyfilla to repair the damage to the plaster."

"Now you're ready to connect the two loose wires to the

screws of the new outlet. Since they're old and frayed, you might want to cut off a bit of the end of each wire and strip back the insulation a few inches."

"Third time's a charm, Dave. Just remember, if you cut off any more of the wire, you won't have enough to attach to the new outlet."

"Whew, that was close, wasn't it Dave?"

"That step was well done. You've pushed the new outlet back into the electrical box and screwed on the faceplate. It looks great. One small problem, though—I don't believe you attached the wires to the new outlet."

"That's right. Just repeat the first three steps then you can attach all the wires. Can I offer some more advice, Dave? You might want to wipe off that sweat dripping from your forehead, as it tends not to mix well with electricity."

"Looking good. Now it's time to reset the breaker and test your work by plugging in the blow dryer and turning it on."

"No, Dave, I don't believe the blow dryer should be smoking. Likewise, I am almost positive that flames should not be coming from the outlet."

"Yes, I have no doubt that you attached both the black wire and the white wire. However, there is a third wire called a 'ground.' No, I didn't think so."

"It's 10 o'clock now, Dave. The flashlights are starting to fade and the flames from the outlet aren't really throwing off enough light to continue working."

"I strongly suggest you defer this project until tomorrow when you can call a qualified electrician. Cost, you ask? Probably about $75 an hour, but that's still less than rebuilding an entire wall."

"OK, suit yourself, Dave. But in all good electronic conscience, I have to shut down now. Before I do, however, I feel obliged to inform you that the number for the ER is 555-5543. And if all else fails, there's always 911."

# Jolt of Reality

by
## Camille DeFer Thompson

"You know the doorbell's not working, right?"

My 18-year-old daughter dropped that little gem on me the day before the open house. I had my eye on a sweet town house near the mall, so I had to make a quick sale of our existing mouse hole. At the advice of my real estate agent, I decluttered by relocating all the unnecessary furniture to my brother's house. I scrubbed, buffed and vacuumed every floor, counter, drawer, shelf and cupboard until my hands bled. Then I tested each light fixture, faucet and drain to be sure all were in peak working order—except, it seemed, the doorbell.

"What?" I said, rubbing Burt's Bees Hand Salve into my palms. "How do you know? Maybe you just didn't hear it."

Kristen rolled her eyes and dragged her fingers through blond tresses.

"Tiffany came over after school last week. She said she tried the bell and it didn't work."

"And you're just telling me now?" I said, gnashing my teeth.

"Yeah, sorry. I guess I forgot."

*Crap*, I said to myself. I had never tackled an electrical issue before. Any fool could dump Liquid-Plumr down a drain or plunge the toilet, but a doorbell? This was a whole new experience.

I couldn't leave it that way. I imagined a potential buyer or agent stopping by for a walk-through. I was pretty sure a non-functioning doorbell would not make the best first impression.

I headed out the front door and started jamming the button with my thumb. *Nothing. This is not happening!* I took a breath then pressed the button again. And again. And again.

Kristen grabbed my arm. "Mom. It's broken. Get over it," she said. "Can I go now?" She stood in the doorway, her hormone-fueled engine revving. A senior on spring break, she had better things to do than fret over home repair.

Growing up, my dad was the handyman. "Guy," my mom would call. "Come look at this light switch. There's something wrong with it." I don't think he ever sought out the professionals. Dad always had the solution to every domicile dilemma. Back then, he spent most weekends sawing in the garage, hammering on the roof or tinkering under the sink. He taught my older brothers all his trade secrets, but excluded me from Home Repair 101. I'm sure this was due, at least in part, to the fact that I lacked the requisite Y chromosome. I grew up believing that home maintenance was a man thing, and that I would never have to worry my pretty little head about such trivial matters.

Then, in my mid-20s, I found myself divorced and caring for a four-year-old on my own. Unwilling to assume the stereotypical role of helpless female, I resolved to become independent.

My passion for self-sufficiency soon turned into an obsession. One time, I was in the middle of hanging new drapery rods when my boyfriend stopped by for dinner.

"Need a hand?" he offered.

"No," I shot back. "I've got this."

The poor guy sat on the couch for an hour, trying to engage me in conversation, while I ranted at the uncooperative hardware. He finally left. I may have lost the guy, but I succeeded in mounting the rods and draperies, though I'll admit they never quite closed right.

But this was different. This was electrical. Electricity can kill you. Never before had household maintenance involved anything lethal. I mustered my feminist fortitude and headed off to Orchard Supply Hardware for a replacement unit.

The greasy-haired associate walked me back to the doorbell display.

"Wow, you know that's electrical, right?" he said, when I picked up the model that looked most like the one I was replacing.

"Yes," I said, fighting the urge to slap those hoops right out of his fat earlobes.

"You know you've gotta cut the power before you start working on it."

I wanted to scream, *Do I look like a space alien?! I found the hardware store, didn't I?!* But I decided against it.

"Really?" I said, feigning helplessness. "You sure?"

"Oh yes, ma'am," he answered, my sarcasm escaping him. "You need to cut the power for sure."

Back home, I identified the appropriate breaker and turned it off. Then I climbed onto the kitchen chair I had positioned under the offending fixture and got to work.

After removing the old chime box, I began to untwist the wiring. "Ouch!" A sharp tingle ran through my finger and up my arm. *Hmmm . . . must be some residual current.*

I heard the front door open and Kristen's backpack hit the floor.

"Ouch! Dammit!" Another jolt got me. "What the . . .?!"

"Mom! Stop!" Kristen yelled, running toward the hall where I was perched, nursing my latest zinger. "You're going to kill yourself! Did you cut the power?" she asked, squeezing past me, on her way to the breaker box.

"Yes! Why does everyone keep asking me that? It was just a little . . . ouch!"

A moment later, the radio went silent and the lights flickered out.

"There," she said, returning from the box. "Now at least you won't kill yourself."

I finished the job in the dim glow of ambient light from the windows. Kristen restored power then headed out to the front porch and put the new doorbell through exhaustive testing.

With the bell check completed, we plopped down together onto the couch and I clicked on the TV. After a moment, Kristen leaned over and gave me a hug. "My mom, the dad!" she proclaimed.

That feeble electric shock I had felt earlier was a mere pin-prick compared with the surge of pride that her words ignited. I realized that the challenges I face as a single parent not only empower me, but demonstrate the strength of independence to my daughter.

"Thanks, kiddo," I said, brushing a strand of hair off her face. "You saved my life."

Kristen smiled and tilted her head to one side. "Yeah, I guess I did."

Ouch! Camille gets another jolt.

# CHAPTER THREE

# The Magic of Wallpaper and Paint

Or not . . .

# Lines and Lions

by
## Laurel McHargue

As far as wives go, I'd say I'm a pretty good one. I'm a decent cook, I've kept us out of debtor's prison and I've even been known to surprise the hubby once in a while. Those surprises were always been greeted with approval . . . until that one day when my quest for drama went a little too far.

Back when decorative wallpaper borders were all the rage and before we even had a home of our own, I had purchased rolls of an exquisite paper decorated with exotic lions and tigers and elephants—oh my!—in rich tones of gold and black and umber. I knew that someday I'd have the perfect room for those wild beasts to hang from.

My animal friends stayed packed away, moving with us each time the Army transferred us to a new location. When we ultimately landed in a home we knew we could live in for many years, I was excited that my safari friends would finally find their new habitat, too, in our spacious master bathroom.

In my mind, I pictured that those lions and tigers and elephants deserved more than just a beige wall to prance around. Our new bathroom was big enough to pull off a dramatic "statement," so with border in hand, I visited our local hardware store.

"I'd like to put this on a color that will really make the animals 'pop,'" I told the pimply paint-counter boy. He nodded and together we studied the colors in the border.

"I think if you put it on this color," he said, pointing to the dark umber, "it'll look cool."

Disregarding the fact that the kid likely had no experience with designing classy interiors, I decided that it would be a daring statement, for sure, and was excited about the idea of going bold with this project. I ordered enough of the earthy paint to cover the bathroom walls, as well as a paint tray and several different brushes. I'd never painted a wall in my life and I wanted this to be perfect. Hubby's a bit of a perfectionist, too, and I wanted to make him proud. And really, how hard could it be?

I didn't tell my man about the master bathroom plan, which included going for a 3-D look by bringing the umber paint 5 inches onto the ceiling and using black to paint ornamental scrollwork up from the corners. I knew it would look totally cool, but I realized it would be a big project and would probably take a few days to complete.

"I'll be going to Germany for a week next month for training," Mike told me one morning over an awesome omelet, one of my specialties.

*Perfect*, I thought, *he'll come home to a wonderful surprise!*

The day after he left, I opened the paint and immediately thought, *YIKES!* The color was darker than I had remembered. But my vision of the completed project moved me to action, and my safari friends were itching to get hung.

I painted the first wall and tried hard to ignore my feelings of panic. My umber was looking far more like baby-shit brown, far less like something I wanted to brush my teeth by each morning. But I persisted. Once I did the 3-D job and got the border up, the paint color didn't look that bad. I just knew that the editors at *Architectural Digest* would send their best photographer out to snap photos of my masterpiece for their world-class magazine.

By the end of day three, I was ready to paint the ceiling border, the one that would make it look like the walls were higher than they actually were. And then the phone rang.

"Hi honey! Just wanted to let you know that our training was cut short and I'll be home tomorrow!" Mike sounded happy. For the first time in our marriage, I wanted him to stay away longer, just long enough for me to finish my masterpiece.

"Yay! Can't wait to see you!" I replied, trying my hardest to sound normal. It would be a long night.

It took me many more back-breaking and neck-straining hours to work my way around the ceiling while standing on the sink counter and ladder. I held a metal yardstick up with my left hand and painted along it with my right, the brown paint dripping onto my face and clothes, as if to say, "Ha! I'm crapping on you!" By 11 P.M., I was beginning to question my sanity. There was no way I would finish the corner scrollwork, let alone hang the border. But I knew that my honey would be able to visualize the final product. It would be fine. Really.

When I woke the next morning and walked into my shit-brown bathroom, I wanted to cry. Mike would be home soon, and I knew that—even if I had completed the project—the whole room would look like hell. But I hoped he would see things differently.

Once home, Mike dropped his bags in the bedroom and I followed him into the bathroom, which, when he had left just days before had been—although beige—still bright and cheerful.

"Umm . . ." he started, looking around the room as if he had just stepped into *The Twilight Zone*, "When you do the final coat, are you going to use a straightedge to make sure the lines are perfectly straight?"

I knew that he was searching for something positive to say, and although "snapped" might not be the perfect word to describe what happened to me next, it'll do. Instead of wailing and gnashing my teeth and beating on his chest while I explained the care I took to ensure precision and excellence, I instead looked at him blankly, smiled and ran downstairs into the basement.

While Mike unpacked and hopped into bed to recover from some serious jet lag, I brought up buckets and buckets of colorful paint from the basement, purchased for our young boys' rooms and basement walls and who knows what other crafty purposes. I decided instantly that by the time I was done with my master bathroom project, there would not be a single straight line in the damn room. I resigned myself to the reality that it was time for my exotic creature border paper to go into the next yard-sale box.

The ceiling was now a baby-blue sky with clouds in the shape of our dog dashing after our delicate koi and the walls had trees climbing up them, their branches reaching up into the "sky" and over the tub. A waterfall crashed over the toilet under a streaking sunset that spread out across the longest wall and covered the back side of the door.

I had never painted anything so daring, so intense, so free-flowing, so crazy, and it felt wonderful. I asked my hubby to refrain from coming into my masterpiece until it was complete, and I think he was more than happy to stay out of my way for the next several days.

Mike finally entered, and I followed him into my exotic new world, closing the door.

"Umm . . ." he started, looking around in what I am telling myself was amazement and delight. Then he looked at me intently.

"Well? What do you think?" I asked with obvious enthusiasm, truly proud of the wonderland mural I had created.

"Good job, dear," he finally said, kissing me on the cheek.

I'm pretty sure what was going through his mind was something more along the lines of, "Oh, my GOD! This is ridiculous!" but he knew that if he had said anything like that, I would have been crushed.

Although my plan of painting the perfect, classy bathroom never materialized, my final product became a conversation piece with friends and family for the years we lived in that wonderful home, and it never failed to surprise all who stepped through that painted doorway.

Laurel's sons in the painted bathroom, Nick (above) and Jake (right)

# Nice Try

by
Harriet Cooper

My once-white kitchen was looking decidedly grubby. It was definitely time for a paint job. As I am anything but handy around the house, having once nearly electrocuted myself on a live wire, I asked my best friend if she knew a good painter who also came cheap. "It's just for the kitchen," I told her.

"Why would you pay someone to paint when you can do it yourself?" Susan asked.

"Because I don't want to do it myself," I said, shuddering at the thought of having to go to the store to buy paint, brushes, paint trays, dropcloths and God knows what else, let alone actually paint. I had memories—well, nightmares might be more accurate—of helping my father do odd jobs around the house. No matter how small the job seemed on the surface, it always meant umpteen trips to the hardware store to pick up something he forgot and took a lot more time and effort than it seemed it was worth.

Unfortunately, Susan wasn't that easily put off. "Don't be such a wuss, Harriet. I've painted most of my house at one point or another. It just takes some planning and a couple of hours. Think of the money you'll save."

"Think of the mess I'll make," I replied. "Besides, I'll probably put my back out painting the ceiling, and then spend the next week in bed."

"Fine," Susan said, "you paint the walls and I'll do the ceiling. I'll pick you up Saturday morning and we'll head to the hardware store and get what we need. A couple of hours of work, and you'll have a bright white kitchen again. And a little extra money in your pocket."

I sighed. "OK, Saturday morning it is."

The next Saturday, we were at the hardware store along with half the homeowners in the city. Susan came prepared with a list of what we needed, including a couple of things I had never heard of. A special tool for corners. Roller frames. Extensions. Liners for roller trays.

Then she got into a long, involved discussion with another weekend painter about the best type of roller to use—ultra weave versus woven mohair versus lambskin shearling. I decided I'd had enough. "I'm heading across the street to the coffee shop. I'll bring you back one."

"But we haven't even picked the shade of white," she said. "Do you want a cool white or a creamy white? We could go antique white, Spanish white, linen white, Dover white . . ."

I held up my hand to stop the flow of words. "Surprise me."

Twenty minutes later when I returned with her coffee, she had filled a cart with enough painting supplies to paint my entire house, plus my neighbor's. "Susan, we're only doing my kitchen. Isn't this a bit much?"

She shook her head. "You'll thank me when it's all done. And a lot of this can be used for another painting job."

*Like I'm ever going to paint again*, I thought. But I plastered a fake smile on my face and handed her a coffee. My smile faltered as we headed to the checkout and the cashier began ringing up the items. As we hit the three-digit mark, I began to wonder how this was saving me money.

Half an hour later we were in my kitchen, surrounded by paint cans, dropcloths and all the other 101 supplies that Susan deemed necessary. She shoved a roll of green tape in my hand. "Start taping the baseboards," she said.

"Huh?" I responded, eying what looked like miles of baseboard. "This is going to take forever. Can't we just paint really, really carefully?"

Susan gave me the look she usually saves for kids who are acting up in her grade-four class. An elementary school teacher, she had the look down cold. "Stop being a pain in the ass. The longer you complain, the longer the job will take. So shut up and start taping."

I taped and taped and taped. "I'm hungry. Can we stop for lunch now?" I whined.

"Not until you've finished taping."

The look I gave her was probably the same look she gets from her school kids. It didn't work. I taped some more.

Finally, everything was taped to Susan's satisfaction. We covered the floor with the dropcloth, stirred the paint and poured some into a lined paint tray. She handed me a roller and pointed to the paint tray. "Work in 3-foot blocks and don't knock over the paint tray." Then she grabbed a second roller with an extension and started on the ceiling at the other end of the kitchen.

I plunged the roller into the tray until it was dripping with paint and attacked the wall, figuring I'd save time by not having to go back to the tray every few minutes.

"Harriet, don't put so much paint on the roller. You'll end up with a very uneven coat with lots of drippy sections."

I closed my eyes, wondering what would happen if I attacked Susan with the roller I now clenched in my hand. All I would need was one person on the jury who had ever painted with a friend or spouse and I'd be acquitted. Hell, I might even get a medal.

Tempting though it was, I sighed to myself and rubbed some of the excess paint off into the tray. Instead, I imagined Susan's face on the wall and painted over it time after time. Not quite as satisfying as attacking her in person, but much safer.

Two hours later, the painting was done. "Now can we eat?" I asked over the grumbling of my stomach.

Susan looked at the painting paraphernalia covering the kitchen floor. "Not until we've cleaned up. A good workman always takes care of his tools."

"Oh, my God, Susan, did you really just say that? You sound like my mother."

She sighed, long and deep, and then turned away to begin the cleanup. The moment her back was turned, I stuck my tongue out at her. I admit it was not the most mature response on my part, but painting the kitchen ourselves had not been my idea.

Once everything was cleaned up and the tape had been

stripped from the baseboards, Susan surveyed our handiwork. "Not bad," she said. "If you don't look too closely, you can barely see some of the streaks from your earlier work. Now isn't this better than hiring someone to paint?"

Then my friend paused. "I noticed your hallway is looking a bit tired. Maybe we can spruce it up with a little paint next weekend. We already have the rollers and trays. Just a little paint and . . ."

"Susan," I interrupted, "I want to thank you for all the hard work you did today. But if you ever suggest we paint anything again, I'll be looking for a new best friend."

She laughed. "OK, forget the hallway. But really, it wouldn't take long."

"Nice try," I said, now brandishing a roller at Susan, "but don't go there. I mean it. Now let's go out for lunch. I'm buying."

As we walked out the door, I wondered how much I could get for all the painting paraphernalia on eBay. Maybe even enough to pay for lunch.

Harriet

# Screw This

by
## MaryAnn Myers

I sat down on the floor and cried. I'd just spent three days wallpapering our new bedroom and was down to the last panel when it all fell apart. I'd wrestled with this stinking wallpaper from day one. Though the perfect color, apparently it wasn't of the finest quality. It liked to stick to itself, to me, to the floor, to the dog.

*Screw this*, I thought.

Top shelf? Of course not. It was on sale and I loved the color, a perfect blend of beige on beige, a tiny flowery pattern. After looking at it for hours and hours all week, I'd decided it actually wasn't flowers I was seeing, but little devil forks instead. Yes, devil forks! Hundreds of them! Thousands of them! All lined up in a row, all perfect in shape, no deviation, all the same, same, same, same. Try lining that up. It's almost impossible. How many rolls? Only 20!

Who would have thought the walls weren't square?

Not me. The room was a brand-new addition. *What the hell!* And did I mention that I was tired of sleeping on the couch? With this new addition, our old bedroom was now a hallway. Yes, it had been a small room, way too small by any standards, but I'm betting it was a perfectly square room. *Plumb.* I hate that word. Chalk lines, don't cross them. WTF?

"Do you want help?" my husband asked.

"No! Did I ask for your help?"

"Nope!"

"Besides, this is all your fault!" I thought back to his pointing out all the wrinkles in that last sheet of wallpaper . . .

"My fault?!" He raised his hands and backed out of the room. The dog followed him.

"That's right, leave!" Yes, I was still sitting on the floor. Yes, I was still crying. I'd gotten so close to finishing and now this. I wiped my eyes, feeling sorry for myself. After all, it's not easy to hang wallpaper. There are all those little air pockets.

"Make a little hole with a sharp razor, a little slit," the man at the wallpaper store told me over the phone. "And then smooth the air out."

That seemed easy enough. But after a few hundred of these annoying little air pockets, my eyes were in danger of becoming permanently crisscrossed.

I asked the man, "Why am I getting all these air bubbles in the first place?" I had used the proper tools, I'd smoothed and smoothed and smoothed.

"Well, madam," the man said on the fifth phone call.

"Madam?"

"Did you treat the walls?"

"Treat them?"

"With sizing?"

"*Sizing?* Are you trying to be funny?"

"No, madam. I don't have a sense of humor. You have to treat the walls."

"With what?"

"Sizing."

I pulled the phone away from my ear and glared at the receiver. I took a deep breath. I gave it another try. "Is there anyone else I can speak with?"

"It's just me and Jim here today."

"Jim?"

"He's in plumbing."

*You've got to be kidding me.* "Never mind." I hung up, heaved a sigh, crumbled onto the floor and stared up at the ceiling. It was a perfect ceiling, all swirly white and thick, like frosting on a cake, whipped cream . . .

"What are you doing?" My husband was back in the doorway again.

"Oh," I said, still lying there gazing up at the ceiling. "Just thinking." I looked at him. "You got a minute?"

He smiled. We've been married a long time. He knows me so well.

"I've got all night," he said.

As he crossed the bedroom, he peeled off his shirt and kicked off his shoes. We crawled onto the bed and he took his time, showing me we indeed had all night. The wallpaper could wait.

In the afterglow, my mind drifted back to that friggin' paper.

*What had my husband said to set me off? "See all those wrinkles?" That was it. What was it . . . minutes . . . hours ago? Maybe it was the critical way he said it, with that I-told-you-so, know-it-all sound to his voice. Perhaps it was his expression.*

My husband interrupted my daydreaming. In a warm and fuzzy voice, he made me an offer. "I'd be happy to remove that sheet of drywall. You could start over. I can help you."

I gave it some thought, still warm and fuzzy myself.

Instead of answering, I jumped out of bed, naked, and yanked that last sheet of wallpaper off the wall so hard and so fast that it tore off half the outside layer of the drywall right along with it.

*That's why you have to treat the wall.* The phrase replayed in my brain. The wallpaper man was right. But tearing off the wallpaper gave me freedom. I mellowed. I regrouped. I crawled back into bed.

The next day I fixed it. I glued the last sheet of wallpaper back onto the wall and if I must say so myself, it didn't look half bad. After all, the pieces of drywall were still stuck to the wallpaper and fit back into place. It looked good until it dried. I hung the drapes—beige satin. I hung the valances. They matched the comforter and pillow shams, the sheets. I was going for the perfect look. I stared. *Why, oh why, does that last sheet of wallpaper have to be smack dab in the center of the room?*

"Because the friggin' walls are not straight," answering my own question, out loud to myself. "It was the only way I could get those friggin' little devil forks to line up straight."

It looked like hell.

Then I had an idea.

The following afternoon, I went back to the store and bought another set of beige silk drapes, valance and a queen-sized comforter. It didn't dawn on me until I got home that I wouldn't be able to hang the curtain rods onto plain old drywall, not to mention adding the weight of a heavy comforter. The rods wouldn't hold. I had holes everywhere!

My husband appeared in the doorway, having just gotten home from work.

"I need a stud finder," I said.

"Oh, babe," he said, with a chuckle. "You are a stud finder."

I laughed. "Do we have one?"

"Yes. Why? What's the plan?" he asked, assessing all the nail holes.

"We're going to hang this comforter on the wall, and we're going to hang drapes over it and tie them back on the sides and we're never ever going to look at this wall again."

He stood there a moment, looking, thinking, and then nodded. "That'll work. That'll look nice. So, you're saying you need my help?"

I smiled. I *am* a stud finder. "Yes. I need your help."

# Caribbean Blue

by
## Pamela Frost

"Yes. I am crazy, but you already knew that. Thanks for asking," I said. My best friend and I were at lunch discussing my latest wild idea.

"I can't believe you want to paint your bedroom turquoise," Donna said over her chicken salad sandwich.

"Not exactly turquoise. I want it to be the color of the Caribbean Ocean."

"You'll never be able to sleep in a room that bright," Donna warned. My beige-loving friend was genuinely concerned about my sleep deprivation.

I was also concerned. *What's Donna thinking?* I asked myself. I had done extensive research on Caribbean Blue. My favorite week of the year is spent frolicking in the radiant blue of the Caribbean Ocean. I love lying under the hot tropical sun, melting into the sand and listening to palm trees rustle in the breeze. Thinking about it now, I could almost taste the salt spray on my lips. No, wait—I was imagining the salt on the rim of a really strong margarita. If only she understood how I adore taking long naps on the beach in my beloved tropical paradise.

*Of course I'll be able to sleep in a room that color.*

Undaunted by Donna's attitude, I cruised paint chip displays all over town, but I couldn't find Caribbean Blue anywhere. It seemed I was on an impossible quest.

It was time for Plan B. I went in search of tropical wallpaper. I discovered the perfect beach-scene border in a store window and was thrilled. But it turned out to be a cruel tease—they only had one roll and I needed six. I could order it, but it would take four to six weeks to arrive.

At our weekly lunch date, I showed Donna the border sample and explained the new plan. "I'll paint the bottom of the wall beige and the top of the wall light blue and run the beach border around the middle. Oh, I could paint the ceiling blue, too."

Donna was enthusiastic. "Order it Pam. It's well worth the wait." I knew she would like this plan since it involved beige.

I whined, "But I really don't want to wait a month for the border."

"No, order it. While you're waiting for the border to come in, you can paint the room," Donna said brightly. Then she declared, "Road trip! Let's go shopping!"

Off we went to Home Depot, the border sample in hand. As I was about to hand it over to the paint technician to have him computer-color-match it for the paint, I noticed a video running about a painting technique using a sponge. It showed how to blend a sky and make clouds. I stood there, transfixed.

"I've got it! I can paint the sky and clouds above the border and paint the bottom half a blended sand color." But in the next instant, I realized the border was not enough. "I could use the border as a sort of pattern and paint the whole room into a beach scene." I could hear angels in my head singing "Hallelujah!"

Donna interrupted my choir with her sarcasm. "You think you can do that? That lady in the video is a real artist. You know it can't be as easy as she makes it look."

"Oh," I sighed, "I can't make up my mind. Let's go to Starbucks and get a Frappuccino to jump-start my creative juices." I was frozen with indecision and feeling kind of blue. Not Caribbean Blue, but the B.B. King kind of blue.

In Starbucks, I plopped down on one of the couches—defeated. I sipped my caramel Frappuccino, letting the caffeine swirl around my brain. I then noticed a shiny travel magazine on the table in front of me, with the perfect Caribbean beach on the cover. It was a sign—it was meant for me.

I picked up the magazine. "This is it! This is what the room has to look like!"

"It's the caffeine talking, honey. Get real. Have you ever painted a mural? Have you ever even painted a picture?"

"Does paint-by-number count?"

"I think you may be biting off more than you can chew. Why don't you sleep on it?" Donna advised. She turned back to her drink, took a sip and delivered what she thought was the clinching blow to the plan. "Whether or not you can do it is immaterial. You haven't been able to find Caribbean Blue paint."

"No, don't you get it? If they can computer-match the color on a sample of wallpaper, why can't they match this?" I asked, holding up the magazine.

When I awoke the next morning, I could still hear Donna's words about biting off more than I can chew and realized she was right. That's me, to a fault. But that magazine—there, on that table, at that time—was a sign. I knew I could do it.

Jumping out of bed, I went to the drugstore to buy a copy of the magazine then straight to Home Depot to buy the paint, the magic sponge and the video. The lady in the paint department had never had a request like mine before. I pointed to different spots on the picture and had her make each color.

I rushed home and started right away. The bottom third of the wall was sand. That part was easy. My confidence soared.

Blending the sky wasn't too hard, but required a little more finesse.

The clouds were impossible. I watched the video over and over. It just couldn't get them right.

I went outside and lay on the deck, studying real clouds. With the image burned into my brain, I charged back upstairs, put on a Bob Marley CD and cranked up the volume.

Sitting cross-legged in the middle of the empty room amid dropcloths and numerous quarts of paint and sipping a cappuccino, I revved myself up. *Just do it! Don't concern yourself with the outcome.* I felt all tingly with energy and excitement. And I painted into the wee hours of the morning.

The room turned out amazing! A couple of wicker chairs, a palm tree in the corner, sheer hibiscus curtains and a tropical print bedspread completed the look. As my Jamaican friends would say, "Ya mon—no problem."

# Coming Unglued

by
Terri Duncan

As a newlywed, I read articles on maintaining a happy marriage. I learned compromise was essential and to never go to bed angry with your spouse. However, nothing provided adequate warning about the dangers of tackling a do-it-yourself project. Therefore, I was totally unprepared for the trauma associated with wallpapering a bathroom. How was I to know a seemingly simple task would wreak havoc on our union?

I was so proud of our new house. The tiny condominium may have appeared cramped to some, but to me it was cozy and romantic. Though our furnishings were sparse and the decorating budget tight, I was perfectly content. However, I soon grew bored with the white walls. A touch of color would certainly be a welcomed respite.

That's when I came up with the brilliant idea to wallpaper the tiny half bath downstairs. The bathroom was so small that I figured it wouldn't cost much to do, and wallpaper would be much cheerier than paint. I was so certain my husband would be as enthralled with the idea as I was that I rushed to the store without consulting him first.

In my haste, I had not taken any measurements or done research on the art of wallpapering. After all, how hard could it be to cut a few strips of paper and glue it to the wall? Why, I was a teacher. I cut and pasted all the time! Thus, with those simplistic notions, I ambled down the store aisle in search of the perfect pattern.

Soon, however, I was overwhelmed by the enormity of the task. Not only were the choices of color and design numerous, but I also had to decide whether to get pre-pasted wallpaper or not. What tools would I need? How many rolls would be necessary? Despite the fact that my brain was becoming frazzled, I would not be deterred. I finally selected two rolls of pre-pasted floral wallpaper with pearly rose-colored stripes. We would have a new look in a matter of hours!

I was waiting at the door with my purchases when my husband came home from work. I eagerly shared my idea. He seemed less than enthusiastic.

"Why'd you have to get pink?" he asked, eyeing my selection with disdain.

"It's not pink," I retorted. "It's rose!"

"Looks pink to me."

The ensuing conversation was not much better. My husband's barrage of questions dampened my enthusiasm considerably. Had I purchased the correct square footage? Did I know how to hang wallpaper? Where were all of the hanging tools? Did we own a ladder? What was wrong with white walls?

"Fine!" I shouted in a huff. "I'll just hang the damn wall-paper myself!" I took a roll under each arm and stomped off.

My husband immediately hopped off the couch and began apologizing profusely. He pried loose the rolls that were now in my clenched fists and agreed that pearly rose-colored striped wallpaper adorned with flowers was perfect. So without further ado, my smile returned, and we started our first do-it-yourself home improvement project.

While my husband read the directions on the label of the wallpaper, I began gathering tools. I located a pair of scissors, a kitchen chair (who needs a ladder?), a rolling pin (it looked like it would serve the same purpose as that little rolling tool described on the wallpaper packaging) and a yardstick that was almost a full yard, except for that broken end piece.

"Well," said my husband, shaking his head at my collection of unique tools, "We still need something to soak the paper in to activate the glue."

I glanced around. "What about the kitchen sink?"

"Too small."

"OK. What about the upstairs bathtub?"

My husband looked skeptical. "We could try that."

I could barely wait to see that splash of color on the walls. Why, if this looked good, just imagine what we could do! I began envisioning the possibilities of flowers, stripes, dots and diamonds on every wall in the house.

It didn't take long for that vision to fade. We realized almost immediately that the two of us could not squeeze into the tiny bath area and still breathe. Therefore, my husband began measuring the wall while I unrolled wallpaper on the den floor. Though I considered myself an expert cutter, I soon realized cutting wallpaper required far more skill than I possessed. It also required special tools, which I had naively assumed were optional.

Nevertheless, I managed to cut a slightly crooked first strip. I raced upstairs to fill the tub and patiently waited as my handyman immersed the wallpaper. As he lifted the dripping paper from the tub, newly wet glue began to ooze onto the bathroom floor.

"You're making a mess!" I screeched, grabbing a towel and feverishly trying to mop up the mess.

"I told you this wouldn't work," he snorted as glue dribbled down his arms.

"Don't you dare get any glue on the carpet!" I called as he began marching down the stairs, grumbling incoherently.

Obviously, this was not going to work. I scrambled to the laundry closet, hoping for an inspiration. *Aha! An ice chest!* I gleefully said to myself upon finding it in the corner. I grabbed it and headed downstairs.

When I reached the bathroom, I saw my very unhappy husband standing on the toilet, covered in floral wallpaper. While he was nicely adorned, the wall was not. I inched my way into the room to offer my assistance.

I learned quickly that a rolling pin is not really adaptable to wallpapering. And he peppered me with more questions, which sent rambling thoughts through my brain: *What did he mean I didn't purchase enough? No, I hadn't considered matching the pattern. You mean I had to buy more of that stuff? What are lot numbers and why does it matter? Take the toilet out to hang behind there? Are you serious?*

For many tumultuous hours, my happy marriage was anything but. While I cried and stomped and made trips to the hardware store, my husband cursed and rolled and glued. Finally having reached my limit, I raced up the stairs, slammed the bedroom door and cried myself to sleep.

Sometime in the wee hours of the morning, my sticky husband crawled into bed.

The next morning, I crept down the stairs before he awoke. As I rounded the corner, scraps of wallpaper and globs of glue greeted me. But then, I walked through the doorway of the tiny half bath. Beautiful floral wallpaper with pearly rose-colored stripes reflected in the mirror! So what if the stripes weren't quite straight. Who cared if some of the seams overlapped just a little? And who was going to look behind the toilet anyway? All of the previous day's home improvement horrors evaporated. I raced upstairs. My new husband and I may have gone to bed angry, but we most certainly were not going to wake up that way.

By mutual agreement, we never again tackled a wallpaper job. For the sake of my marriage, I learned early on I needed to avoid sticky situations. After all, I don't want any seams to ever come unglued again!

# When the Wife's Away

by

## John Reas

I really don't like to paint. It's one of those brainless, do-it-yourself chores that require some level of attention to detail to ensure that the paint is applied to the destination I have in mind.

But painting the exterior of a home isn't too bad. At least in that situation, I'm outside in the sun. The job only requires simple motor skills to cover the edifice with the desired look without being too fearful of the paint landing where it isn't wanted. After all, I can mow the lawn or trim the bushes to get rid of the spills that typically accompany those painting episodes. But any work that entails the interior? That's a totally different scenario.

First, there's the hassle of moving the furniture to make room for the operation. This is followed by taping the floor and ceiling molding then putting down dropcloths to protect the carpet, which never seem to quite cover the area. Murphy's Law of Sherwin-Williams dictates that the one small square inch of exposed carpet that the dropcloth doesn't cover will be the one spot in the entire room where paint splatter will land. If anything is true in my life, I am a stickler for following laws, especially those written by Murphy.

Still, as far as home improvement projects are concerned, painting is something that I feel reasonably competent enough to accomplish—without making it a total disaster. The way I see it, if a mistake was made, I'd just cover it up. It is the perfect solution for a do-it-yourselfer wannabe like me.

When we built our home in Texas, the walls were painted beige. My wife, Helen, and I thought it was pretty bland, particularly in the living area where we spent most of our time. So, after a trip to Home Depot, we brought back several color samples and settled on a nice hunter green for the main living room. After a long weekend, with a few errant drops on the carpet that were quickly cleaned up, we both settled back and admired our handiwork.

A few years later, I noticed that a small sliver of paint on the wall separating the living room from the kitchen had chipped off. How the paint chipped in the first place was never determined, although I suspected it was probably when I was moving a table one day and accidentally bumped into the wall without noticing. To me, it looked like the entire wall was now marred with the offending original beige color daring to break through to the surface.

"Great. Just look at this. Now we'll have to repaint the entire living room," I muttered.

"It's not that noticeable," Helen replied. "Don't worry about it."

"No, I think I need to just patch it up. It won't be a problem," I insisted.

"Well, we don't have any leftover paint, and I want to make sure the color matches," she said. "We can worry about it after next week." She was taking the kids to Louisiana over the weekend, with her sister and her niece coming home with her Sunday afternoon.

Friday night after work, I returned home to a quiet house, made my way to the fridge and pulled out a cold beer. Then I went into the living room and turned on the TV. My eyes wandered over to the wall with the offending chipped paint, and I decided then and there that I could get this taken care of before Sunday afternoon.

I quickly changed, drove to Home Depot and brought back color charts. Proceeding through an amazing selection of different shades of green, I settled on one that I was convinced would match.

The next day, after running other errands, I went back to the store to pick up the custom-tinted paint.

"How much do you need?" the paint guy asked.

"No more than a pint," I replied. "It's just a touch-up job. I don't have any leftover paint from before, but I know that this is a dead match."

After he mixed up the right shade for me, I picked up a couple of brushes and a paint tray and headed home to what I believed to be a 30-minute job.

After the first strokes of the brush, I noticed the color

seemed to be slightly lighter than the surrounding wall. *It's got to be the lighting in the room,* I thought to myself. *I'm sure it'll be OK after it dries.*

When I finished, I went outside to do some yardwork and came back into the house an hour later. Much to my dismay, the paint had dried to a lighter finish. *How could I have been so off on the color selection?* Now I had a wall of hunter green with an irregular looking patch of pea green that was impossible to ignore.

I pulled out the color charts and once again looked through the samples. *Ahh,* I thought. *Here's the one. Dead match.*

I jumped into the car and once again went to Home Depot. The same paint technician was there and looked up as I approached the counter. "I was off with the color selection before. This one is definitely a match," I said, trying to act as nonchalantly as possible.

The technician looked at me skeptically, "You know, you've got be careful when matching colors. It's best to do it in as much natural light as possible. Are you sure that this is the right color?"

"No doubt! One pint will do the trick!" I felt confident.

After leaving the store, I stopped by Burger King for a quick lunch. I planned to catch a film later with a buddy, but planned on painting first before meeting him.

Arriving home, I quickly popped open the can of paint and liberally applied it to the wall. *Hmmm, it looks darker than the earlier paint.* I quickly cleaned up and went out to the movies, fully confident the mission was accomplished.

By the time the movie let out and we had a bite for dinner, it was late evening when I returned home. As I flipped on the lights in the living room, I stopped dead in my tracks. Now, instead of pea green, the patched paint was a darker forest green that definitely stood out from the rest of the wall.

I was about to croak. *This isn't working. I'm not colorblind. How could this happen twice?!*

I grabbed the color samples yet again and went through them all. I finally found the shade of green that exactly matched the rest of the wall in the bright lights of the living room.

Looking down at my watch, I realized Home Depot was still open. I jumped back into the car and went for what had to be my final trip to get the paint that would put an end to this madness.

The store was nearly deserted when I entered. The paint guy who had twice offered me helpful advice earlier that day had been replaced by a bored-looking youth with a pimply face.

"Yeah, whatcha' need?" he yawned.

"Just get me a gallon of this, please." I decided not to take any chances this time and would paint the whole damn wall to ensure I wouldn't have to make any return trips.

Once home, I was determined to finish this job once and for all. I found some masking tape, laid out dropcloths and removed the wall outlet plates. Then I carefully pried open the paint, convinced that I had finally matched the color.

Two hours later, I looked at the wall with complete satisfaction. *Finished—at last!* When my wife returned, I could proudly showcase my successful painting job. Even Michelangelo couldn't have felt more pleased after completing the ceiling of the Sistine Chapel.

The next day—Sunday—was a blur. I left the house early for church without stopping to check on my work in the living room. It was shortly after the Sunday worship that my cellphone rang.

"We're on the road, heading back," my wife called to say. "We should be home in an hour."

"OK. I'm going out to grab brunch with a couple guys here, but will be home around the time you arrive." I hung up, looking forward to how pleased she would be to see the wall freshly painted.

About an hour and a half later, I pulled into the garage. The first person to greet me was my 14-year-old niece, who promptly blurted, "Nice job with the wall, Uncle John."

I looked at her in surprise, and then in alarm, as she added, "Not."

I walked into the living room and looked at the wall in horror. There, defying me once and for all, was not the hunter green that adorned the other walls, but the unique color that belonged to the Green Bay Packers' football jersey.

Helen glared at me from the living room sofa. "So, you couldn't just wait until I came home and went with you to match colors?" she asked.

Her sister came into the living room, and repeating her daughter's comment, simply said, "Hey, John. Nice paint job."

I tried to think of a good excuse and lamely came up with, "Don't you think that this adds character to the room? I do. Think of the conversation piece we now have whenever we have guests over."

Her sister laughed and my wife just shook her head.

I offered, "You know, I still have some of that gallon left over. You want me to paint the hallway?"

"No!" she shrieked. "I think that's enough for today."

With that, I was relieved of all painting duties in the house. Come to think of it, it was a pretty smooth way not to be assigned that type of work in the future.

After all, as I stated earlier, I really don't like to paint.

John and the infamous wall

# The Perils of Paint

by

## Mary Mendoza

My husband, the Rembrandt of home renovators, loves to paint. For him it's deeply satisfying to guide a paint roller across uncharted territory. He thrills to the feel of a hog-bristle brush in his hand. He loves to dapple, spackle, putty and prep. He's mesmerized by drips.

So when I suggested we paint and redecorate our son's room, he didn't give me his usual lecture about fiscal management and cost overruns. It was obvious to the both of us that the Ninja Turtle décor in the kid's room was past its prime. After all, he's in junior high school now. Since I hate to paint, my duties were to pick out the paint color and come up with a brilliant decorating scheme. It was the perfect job for me, combining my hen-pecking skills with my gift for design.

Indecision immediately had me in its evil clutches when it came to the decorating scheme. Did we want a rustic-cabin-in-the-woods motif? Should we go for the timeless appeal of

Elvis? Maybe a *Lord of the Rings* theme? Perhaps a nature mural or seascapes stenciled across the walls? I didn't want to get sucked back into the insomnia and insanity of the *Zorba the Greek* living room curtain fiasco of a few years ago. This time, I'd be calm and rational.

First, I had my husband remove the unsightly miniblinds that had hung on the windows since 1960. Common sense dictated silk shantung drapes with gold-leaf tiebacks were ill advised in a room that serves as a hideout from parents and a repository for electronic gadgets. As I debated the virtues of Roman shades versus textured sheers, my husband's eyes started to glaze over. Our son didn't care—an old sheet over the curtain rod would work for him.

After an exhaustive search, I found some wooden curtain rods in fake maple that matched his antique bed and dresser. Three weeks and four return purchases later, I settled on a pair of tab-top curtains. They weren't exactly what I wanted, but would do until the real thing came along.

I yearned to replace the worn comforter and bed skirt with Belgian linens, but settled for a muted macho-plaid Martha Stewart comforter, matching sham and dust ruffle. So much for trying to wean myself off Martha's products—she's just so darn good at what she does.

Then I turned my attention to the paint. The white walls had to go, but because the room is small, a dark color was out of the question. I also had to match the curtains and bed linens. I entered the paint section of Home Depot full of optimism, only to have my hopes dashed when the clerk refused to become embroiled in my decorating problems. I was alone in my quest, adrift on a sea of colors. Choices ran the gamut from antique alabaster to zany zephyr, from romantic Renaissance to *Brady Bunch* retro.

Finally, and with great trepidation, I chose a blue-green shade called "Sea Foam."

Finally, painting day arrived. I assembled the troops for a pre-painting pep talk. "OK, repeat after me. Paint is our friend. Paint is here to help us. We are not intimidated by paint."

"Do I hafta, Mom?" the kid whined.

My husband glared at me. "Step aside and let me at it!"

During the next few hours, I pointed out spots my husband missed, critiqued his work and performed other supervisory duties. When I became entangled in the dropcloth and accidentally brushed against wet paint, I was asked to leave.

When the job was complete, my husband called me back to admire his work.

"It looks different than it did in the store," I said.

"You picked the color," my husband replied.

"It's OK, Mom, I like it," said my adorable son.

"It's so *Miami Vice*! So Santa Barbara, so French Riviera!" I wailed. "What have I done?!"

The next day, still overwrought but trying to be adult, I re-examined the room. That's when I noticed the paint around the mirror attached to the closet door was still tacky. My finger left an imprint. Before I could stop myself, I removed the mirror and started peeling away the paint. Some of it came off easily in long leathery strips and other sections were dry and granite-like.

I scraped away, burrowing through four layers of paint until

I reached what was the original 1940s-era primer. The door now resembled the landscape on Mars—crater-like, scabby, desolate.

I sent the kid to the garage for the electric sander. After hours of backbreaking toil, it occurred to me that sanding was ineffective on semi-wet paint.

"Paint remover. That's what I need," I told the kid.

"Mom, you better let Dad do it."

"I do NOT want your father involved. I've got to fix this before he gets home."

Around 4:30, almost overcome by fumes and covered with gritty gunk, I summoned the kid again.

"An acetylene torch. That's what I need. Get the phone book and look up 'equipment rentals.'"

"Geez, Mom, you want to burn down my room? Let's wait for Dad!"

When my husband arrived home, I was close to tears. The closet door and I both looked like extras in a horror movie.

"What in hell happened?" he asked.

"I was just doing a little touch-up work, darling, when things got a bit out of hand."

My husband spent the rest of the evening repairing the damage. The next day, he moved the sander and painting supplies to an undisclosed location and informed the equipment rental place not to take my calls.

Happily, the color has started to grow on me and my husband is fully recovered from this painful paint experience. I gained wisdom and insight, too. I learned it's not easy being Rembrandt's assistant.

# Steamed

by
### Lesley Morgan

My 81-year-old mother needed to sell our ancestral home and move to a smaller, less-isolated place. So we contacted our town's most prestigious real estate diva, who just happened to work for the same firm as my mother's know-it-all, recently retired neighbor.

On her first visit to our house, the diva was unimpressed. Her face bore a polite but pained expression, as if her pantyhose were too tight. On her second visit, the diva brought her stager. They were brutal as they numbered the shortcomings of our quasi-neglected abode. The estimate for "cosmetic upgrades" totaled almost $13,000. At the top of the list was that the dining room wallpaper "MUST GO." This saddened my mom, who loved the sunny yellow chrysanthemum-and-canaries paper that had grown creamy with age. Installed soon after my parents moved into the house, those birds had witnessed 45 years of family celebrations. But the diva demanded neutral paint, so neutral it would be.

Once my mother had recovered from the $13,000 sticker shock, she was anxious to get the house on the market as economically as possible. To save money, we decided to fix whatever we could ourselves and avoid hiring the stager. The diva was disappointed and was replaced by us with an upbeat agent from a different firm. Meanwhile, I decided to tackle the dining room's walls where two layers of paper—one that was 60 years old under another that was 40—both clung to the plaster for all they were worth.

First, I sponged a hot, steamy solution of vinegar and water onto a small section of wall. I let it sit for a minute. Then, with my trusty Five-Way Wonder Tool, I attempted to scrape off the old paper. I had had success with this technique in the past. However, in this case, it went nowhere. It was like trying to move the Rock of Gibraltar with a toothpick.

I strongly believe that every girl should have a Five-Way Wonder Tool. I keep mine tethered to my hip next to my Swiss Army survival tool. Still, I needed something more powerful to subdue the Wallpaper from Hell, so I went to the hardware store for a Tiger Paw and some DIF wallpaper remover.

A Tiger Paw conjures something a lot more romantic and dangerous than a geared knob with petite, wheeled teeth. When lightly scrubbed in a circular motion, the tool perforates the surface of the wallpaper. This prep makes the wallpaper so susceptible to the DIF and warm water cocktail that the paper relaxes and can be easily removed. I practically poured the DIF mix onto the walls, hoping that the paper would fall down drunk. All I managed to do was to revive the bursitis in my shoulder before my tennis elbow flared up.

My mother became my assistant. Short of chewing the paper off the wall, we tried every possible means of cajoling the golden, floral-dotted-with-birds paper down from its perch. I had envisioned neat sheets rolling off the walls like a troupe of well-rehearsed acrobats. Instead I got shreds—a zillion of them—which was the wall-waste of unprimed plaster and an abundance of glue. With two of us working, the take-down crawled at a painful pace. We finally relented and traveled across town to rent a mammoth steamer, which I quickly nicknamed "The Beast."

The Beast was a 30-pound behemoth that resembled a giant's steel lunchbox, complete with the domed top that could accommodate Joe Construction's full-size thermos. It was stickered all over with an assortment of cautionary exclamations in three languages: HOT! CHAUD! CALIENTE! Furthermore, the Beast was accessorized with enough hose to perform a colonoscopy on an elephant, a steam paddle perfect for spanking an unruly child or kinky sex partner and a steam bar that resembled a conventional power strip. The rental-store clerk threw in a medieval torture device—a cylindrical Mace on a stick—which was intended to maul the paper right off the wall.

There was no manual to tell us how to unleash the Beast. He came with minimal instructions pasted to his flanks in French, Spanish and English. The gist of it was not to overfill, wait 30 minutes before use and never let the Beast run dry. Somehow I hefted the Beast to the kitchen sink and filled its belly with steaming hot tap water. My mother offered a recently shrieking, roiling tea kettle with her deepest condolences. "I'm so sorry you have to work this hard." I heard this refrain often during the next three days.

Working with the Beast was neither pleasant nor easy. With understated good intentions, the rental clerk had told us to plan for some moisture at the beginning. So I positioned the Beast on a rubber-backed welcome mat. Unfortunately, the clerk made no mention of rivulets running down the steam arm, my arm or the wall. I was quite dismayed to see little geysers spring forth from the waffle-iron-sized paddle I had seized for the main event. I commandeered all of my mother's ancient bath towels and left a swath of soaking terrycloth in my wake as I spent hours doing a shuffling sidestep of steam and scrape.

By sunset, I had removed mountains of disintegrating paper, baring plaster as smooth as a baby's bottom that had been creamed with wallpaper paste. Being too tired to tackle the areas above the doors and below the windows, I left some work for the following day. That's when I learned that, despite appearances, the longer, skinny steam bar was far more difficult to brandish than its paddle-shaped cousin. The hose-bearing end defied all balance, making it a struggle to hold it against the wall for hours on end. I persevered, however, stripping my last floral shred at the crack of noon, after which the Beast was returned to its rental lair.

My next two days were filled with patching, priming and painting the walls with a lovely, neutral ivory color that was chosen after hours of painful deliberation. The whole process was grueling and oddly funny. At least, that was my impression as I stood over the stationary sink, (honestly, that's what my mother calls it, as if it might choose to walk off on its own), giving a hand job to the paint roller slated for reuse after a day of priming. At the end of the week, however, the dining room was blandly beautiful in a way that only realtors can love. And knowing that we had saved a considerable chunk of the $13,000, we poured each other a large glass of wine and toasted to our success.

Dining room, sans wallpaper

# CHAPTER FOUR

# Go with the Flow

A straight flush beats a full house every time!

# Where Real Men Hang Out

by
## Ernie Witham

New Year's resolutions never seem to work out for me. For example, a few years ago, I resolved to make the workplace better for everyone by offering my boss a few timely suggestions on how to run the organization more efficiently. I've been gainfully unemployed ever since.

Then last year, I resolved to lose 10 pounds. Instead, I ended up gaining 15.

And this year, I promised my wife I would devote more time to home improvement. It was either that or agree to attend more cultural events. How was I to know she'd want to start improving things immediately?

My daydreaming was interrupted by a professorial-looking guy wearing a corduroy blazer. He was seated right beside me. "If it was up to me, I'd go with the bold look of Kohler in rainforest green," he said.

We were sitting on model toilets in the bathroom display

section at Home Depot, perusing the store's latest catalog. Our significant others scoured the various sections for impossible-to-resist, after-Christmas bargains being announced periodically over the public address system:

"Attention! Now on aisle 27: scum-resistant shower curtains. Buy two, get one free."

"While you're there, look for Fit and Trim, the vanity mirror that takes off 10 pounds. We'll take off $10."

"And be sure to visit the lawn and garden section for 5 gallon jugs of Catch-o'-the-Day fish emulsion fertilizer, now available with a handsome sea-bass-shaped trowel."

There were a number of other guys settled in on the adjacent model toilets, plus a few guys with Home Depot catalogs tucked under their arms, waiting for an opening. After all, there was no sense trying to concentrate on catalog perusal without being in the usual catalog-perusing position.

"I like the rainforest green one, too," another guy said, peering over the top of his reading glasses. "But what about this loganberry-colored one I'm on? Now this toilet makes a statement."

"My wife would never go for a red toilet," a beefy guy at the opposite end of the row said sadly. "She'd probably wanna go with beige."

I felt his pain. The chances of talking my wife into a colored toilet were about the same as the chances of getting a special-order padded seat with built-in climate control to go with it.

We all turned the page.

"Here's something," I said. "A he-man-sized Jacuzzi tub

with sensual-fingers massaging jets."

"Oh yeah, wouldn't that feel good after a grueling day of football," beefy-guy said longingly.

"You bet," chimed in a short guy who was seated on a "Daydream Blue" American Standard. "My back is always killin' me after five or six hours on the couch. Not to mention that carpal tunnel thing from using the remote."

"Well, you're all in luck," I said. "This weekend, it's 40 percent off. And, it says here, they're easy to install."

There was a moment of silence—then we all laughed.

"I got a garage full of easy-to-install stuff," the guy with the reading glasses said.

"Me, too," added the American Standard guy. "Matter of fact, I've got an easy-to-install garage door opener in my garage."

"How does it work?" I asked.

"Danged if I know. I never got around to installing it."

"Hey. Check it out. Page six," beefy-guy piped up. "They got one of those shoe organizers on sale. You know, for the closet. I'm thinkin' that would make a great Valentine's Day gift. Whataya think?"

"Great idea," several of us said, circling it in our catalogs.

"We're being signaled," said one of the standing husbands. His comment turned our attention to a woman holding a complex-looking faucet. She was waving from a green granite faux kitchen just two aisles over.

It was my wife. "Oh, man," I said. "Look at all those fittings." Reluctantly, I stood and headed her way.

"Tough break, fella," a husband with long white sideburns

said, taking my place on the toilet. Then he asked the others: "What page we on?"

"Fourteen. Fashionable shades and vertical blinds," one of them answered.

I walked over to my wife and kissed her on the cheek, just as she handed me something called a "Deluxe Dual Tap with Multi-Function Sprayer." I thought about my last home plumbing project and how long it took the house to dry out. It was then I realized I probably should have chosen the culture event choice for my New Year's resolution.

# What Comes Around Goes Around

by
## Pamela Frost

Some days, it just doesn't pay to answer the phone, especially when you're a landlord. I was playing *Words with Friends* and answered without looking at the caller ID. Big mistake.

Her southern drawl unmistakable, it was Lottie. "Miss Pam, I gots a problem with the toilet. It be leakin' through the dining room ceiling a little bit. I been putting Drano down it, but nothing be happening."

I groaned and massaged my temple. "I'll be right there," was all I could say. As a landlord, I knew going over there would be a challenge—with Lottie and her young kids, every trip was a surprise, and many times, it wasn't a good surprise.

Upon arrival, the first thing I noticed was a huge chunk of plaster sagging in the dining room, just moments away from falling. Under that, a bucket sat atop the dining room table. Dirty dishes from the family breakfast still sat on the table next to the bucket that was catching overflow from the toilet.

I looked away in disgust.

My blood pressure was on the rise. I asked Lottie, "Does the toilet leak all the time or just when you flush it?"

"I don't know," was her reply. "I turned the water off to the toilet."

I tried to control myself, but it was hard not to give her the eye-roll thing. I thought, *How could she not know when it leaks?* Then I noticed the faint smell of marijuana in the air and got a clue.

I went upstairs to find piles of smelly wet towels all around the base of the toilet. I donned my latex gloves and began to sling them into the tub. While bent over, I noticed that one of the toilet bolts was completely missing. It was certainly no mystery why water was coming through the dining room ceiling. I lifted the lid and it was all I could do to keep from vomiting. It was full of shit, a brown puree with a few solid logs.

I ran from the bathroom, gagging. I stood in the hall and thought about calling a plumber—it would be worth whatever they charged not to have to deal with this. But I was low on funds. *Damn!* As I headed to my truck for parts, I tried hard to think about all the money I was saving by fixing the toilet myself. Needless to say, a little pep talk was in order to get me back into the house and up those stairs. And a prayer, as well.

Returning, I passed through the living room on the way upstairs. There sat Lottie, casually watching TV. I wasn't sure where her bratty kids were, and I didn't ask—at least the house was somewhat quiet for me to get my work done without the children bothering me.

Instead, I asked Lottie how long the toilet had been loose.

"Oh, is it loose?" she said.

*Ugh!* I was rapidly approaching hopping mad. But I knew I had to maintain a calm appearance. If I let go of my tight rein, I would have to kill someone.

Back upstairs, I carefully eased the toilet off the remaining bolt, trying to keep it level so as not to spill the contents. After that, I poured a bucket of water into the hole in the floor and found the water flowed freely.

That told me it was the toilet that was clogged, not the pipes. I set up new bolts and eased the toilet back into place. In an effort to break up the turd jam, I poured water into the bowl a little at a time to avoid overflow. I then plunged and snaked and added more water, managing to force enough water through so what was left in the bowl was now nearly clear water. But the snake wouldn't go all the way, and I knew it would clog again as soon as I left.

I took the toilet back off and lay it on its side, placing the wet towels back on the floor to catch the water. The bottom was packed with shit, but by now, I was getting immune to the entire scene.

I tried to force the snake in from the bottom. It jammed again and came back dripping. I tried to poke a coat hanger in, but the toilet seemed to have something solid wedged about half way in. On my way out the door to find something stiffer to ram into the toilet, I remarked to Lottie, "I think something is jammed in there, maybe a toy, I've seen it happen before."

"Oh, I can see how that might happen, and I'm sure it'll happen again," was all she said. At that point, I exited the domicile rapidly to keep from strangling the woman.

*It'll happen again. It'll happen again. It'll happen again.*

Lottie's words ran through my head over and over as I stormed out to my truck. The words made me fume. Her attitude made me want to smack her upside the head. She didn't care that her family ate breakfast from a table with a toilet bucket on top. She didn't care that the ceiling was about to fall. She didn't care that the bathroom smelled like an outhouse.

*She let this go on for weeks, knowing there might be a toy in there! Did she really think Drano was going to dissolve a toy?* I was tempted to get in my truck and leave. If she didn't care, why should I? But reason set in—she was trashing my house trying to flush a clogged toilet, so I had no choice. I had to fix it.

I couldn't find anything else in the truck to jam into the toilet, so I went back to work ramming the snake into it from one side then the other, but nothing was happening. I tried and tried and tried.

Lottie left for work. Again, no idea where the kids were, but at this point, I didn't care. I had had enough and needed a break. I closed the door behind me and went to get something to eat. I couldn't believe I could think about food after being up to my elbows in shit all afternoon, but I hadn't eaten all day and it was getting late.

When I got back from wolfing down a Whopper, I decided to tip the toilet upside down in the bathtub and run water through it backward. It seemed like a great plan at Burger King. But I forgot to factor in how heavy the toilet was and that a true sadist laid out the bathroom. The toilet was jammed in between the wall and the sink, with no room to spare.

Rethinking the logistics, I figured out I would have to lift the toilet up and over the sink vanity to get in into the bathtub.

Determined, I rolled it this way and that, trying to get a grip on the damn thing. But I couldn't. And the last of the water in the bowl was running out all over the place. *Crap!* Literally.

After a few more tries, I was mad enough and had enough adrenaline flowing that I felt like Ms. Incredible Hulk. So with all my might, I tried to lift it. Then I dropped it. As I looked down at the mess I'd made, I knew I was surely going to have to burn my pants and shoes when this repair from hell was over.

I gave up. Since it was getting late, I decided to put the toilet back on, and then leave Lottie a note that I'd be back with a new toilet the next day.

Struggling to flip the toilet back upright and get it lined up over the hole and onto the new bolts, it finally I dropped into place. And that's when I saw it. A flash of yellow in the toilet bowl. *What's that?* My instinct was to reach down and jerk whatever it was out before the big bad toilet sucked it back up into itself again. But I quickly snapped my hand back because the toy was covered in you-know-what.

Slapping on some new latex gloves, I reached in to extract the culprit. The thing was big and hard to maneuver, but it finally came free. It was a little Weeble toy—a guy in a yellow boat had been at the heart of a turd jam for at least two weeks.

I leaned on the wall and breathed a sigh of relief. Evil Pam wanted to take the boat down and put it on top of the TV or the dining room table. But Nice Pam flipped it into the bathtub on top of the soggy towels. Then I left Lottie a note saying I'd return tomorrow to fix the ceiling.

Throwing a tarp over the truck seat, I headed home. When I got there, I didn't care how cold it was—I took my pants and shoes off on the porch and left them. After a long hot shower, I took a long bathtub soak in fragrant bubbles then another shower before climbing into bed.

In my dreams, I saw myself as a child being punished for playing in the toilet. It wasn't that far off, because as a kid, I had done this. In my dream, my father was on his knees in the bathroom for hours, using a coat hanger to unclog the toilet. There was lots of shouting going on, even though he was alone in the bathroom. My punishment was the belt across my legs.

Then I saw myself watching a little boat swirling around with the flush. Traveling round and round, finally disappearing. That's when I knew karma is a bitch—what comes around goes around.

Landlord Pamela, in true "plumber fashion," demonstrating how to lift a toilet, and another toilet in need of some TLC, minus the "C."

# The Domino Effect

by
Banjo Bandolas

If nothing else, experience has taught me that any seemingly harmless little job should be viewed with utmost suspicion. Considering my history of home and automotive repair catastrophes, I really should have known better.

You've probably heard of the less-than-completely-scientific principles of Murphy's law: "Anything that can go wrong will go wrong." Well, Murphy's law has a kissing cousin called the "Domino Effect" which, through chain reaction, can turn any repair endeavor into enough work to make a battalion groan.

Recently, I tempted fate once again and paid the price. It all started out so innocently. My wife, Bonne, noticed a small leak in the bathroom. Knowing that water leaks can be very damaging, a fact she had learned by voraciously reading various technical magazines like *Home & Garden* and *Martha Stewart's Living*, she immediately marched into the family room to inform the maintenance department. Me.

I was right in the middle of my favorite weekend activity—inactivity. I tried not to whimper as she gave me that I-got-a-job-for-you look.

"I need you to look at something!" she said, positioning her body strategically in front of the television, hands planted defiantly on each hip.

"Now?" I asked, twisting to see the screen. It was my standard reply to most demands placed upon my all-important relaxation time. The word had served me well in the past, allowing me to put off hundreds of hours of work.

"Yes, now!" she said, rolling her eyes. "Water's coming out from under the toilet when I flush it. We need to get it fixed before the whole floor caves in."

"I'll take a look at it later. Sounds like the wax seal needs to be replaced," I said, waving her away from in front of the TV. "I'm kinda busy right now."

Bonne turned and looked at the TV then swung back to me. "Is that reeeeeaaaaally important?" she asked, pointing at the program I was watching.

"Well," I squirmed, feeling like an ant under a magnifying glass on a sunny day. "Uh . . ."

Bonne fixed me with a silent glare that'd make a prison guard shudder.

"I guess it wouldn't hurt to take a quick look at it now."

In the bathroom, under Bonne's intense supervision, I flushed the toilet. A dribble of water escaped from under the base. "See what I'm talking about?" she said, pointing at the fluid. "Let's call the plumber."

"The plumber?" I responded, miffed by her suggestion. "You want me to call a plumber to replace a $1 part? I'm not going to pay some plumber $130 to put in a $1 part! I'll do it myself."

"Ack!" Bonne shrieked, an obvious overreaction to my DIY announcement. "I mean, are you sure that's what you want to do? Remember, we have guests showing up tomorrow."

"Don't worry. I'll be done in plenty of time," I said, walking to the storage room to retrieve my tool box. Bonne followed me.

"Be careful. Remember what happened last . . ."

"I thought we weren't going to talk about that anymore?" I reminded her as I entered the room.

"I know, it's just . . ."

"Don't you have some shopping to do or something?" I asked indignantly, pulling out my battered tool box. "I'll have this all finished by the time you get back."

"Promise?" she responded nervously, looking from me to the tool box and back again.

I silently answered her with what I hoped was a withering stare. Eighteen years of marriage had obviously blunted my once-powerful and frightening bug-eyed, get-lost face because Bonne simply shrugged it off with a nonchalant, "Whatever." She collected her purse and keys. "I'll take my time, so don't feel pressured," she called from the door as she left.

"Fine!" I grunted, feeling and looking very caveman-like as I squatted in front of the tool box, digging for an adjustable wrench in the greasy tangle of tools. I located it and held it up for inspection, grunting in my best caveman voice, "Ummm, good wrench. Oook! Fix toilet! Arrrrrg!"

I approached the bathroom confidently, trying not to show any fear. Plumbing, like dogs, can smell weakness in a man. Once the stale scent of fear is detected, the subtle, insidious attacks begin. Maybe that's why plumbers always get the problem fixed the first time. They don't know the meaning of fear—or how to spell it, in some cases.

Perhaps if it hadn't been my bathroom, I would have stood some sort of chance. Knowing me as well as it did, I had about as much chance of making it through this job unscathed as I would have running through a blackberry patch naked. I was doomed and too dumb to know it.

Steeling myself, I reached down to grip the tarnished chrome handle of the inlet valve to the toilet. It crumpled in my hand like a discarded eggshell. I stifled a whimper and retreated to the tool box for the proper weapon . . . er . . . tool. Armed with a pair of pliers, I returned and assaulted the valve stem in its cramped little hidey-hole behind the stool. It was frozen, of course. I had to blindly grip the metal shaft and pull, a quarter turn at a time, until I finally managed to close it. *OK, I thought as I began creating a list on the back of a discarded envelope, I need a new valve handle and a wax gasket. That's not too bad.*

Scooping and flushing, I emptied as much water as I could from the tank. I disconnected the feeder pipe, which, taking instruction from the valve handle, promptly turned to scrap metal at my touch. *OK, I need to add a feeder hose to the list.*

Thankfully, the cap nuts holding the toilet to the floor decided to cooperate and spun off with little resistance. Our bathroom is very narrow, with the sink and toilet on one side, the bathtub on the other and a narrow walkway in between. I stood there and scratched my head, trying to decide where to place the toilet once I had removed it from the mounts. *Of course!* I thought in a light-bulb moment. *The bathtub!* The tub would be the perfect place—if there were any water left in the toilet, it would harmlessly drain into the tub without making a mess. To protect the finish in the tub, I scrounged up some cardboard and placed it inside. I then kneeled down to grab the toilet.

You know, there really isn't a good way to pick up a toilet by yourself. No matter how you grab it, you end up with your face positioned where a face doesn't belong. I don't care how well the porcelain's been scrubbed; it will never seem entirely clean when you consider its history.

Shaking off such wimpy thoughts, I psyched myself up for a clean-and-jerk lift, just ak a weight lifter does when facing those impossibly heavy barbells. Bending down, I caught the base of the stool with one arm and balanced the weight of the tank with the other. What happened next is not for the faint of heart.

I stood up straight, holding the throne. It wasn't nearly as heavy as I thought it would be. Slowly, I turned toward the tub. Halfway through my turn, the toilet decided to unburden itself of whatever effluent remained hidden in its mysterious chambers. A gush of what I could only imagine was the most disgusting water on earth soaked the front of my pants and the bathroom floor. In my haste to get the toilet over and into the tub, I lost my balance and dropped it. The porcelain-on-porcelain contact screamed with a sickening *crunch!* as the toilet shattered and made a large divot in one side of the bathtub then tumbled to make two more in the bottom and the back. *Feeder hose, valve handle, wax gasket, one brand-new toilet and some porcelain patch. This is getting expensive.*

As I cleaned up the water on the floor, I realized how old and weathered the linoleum looked. I remembered the wood-grain peel-and-stick tile squares I'd purchased on sale a few years back, and then had promptly forgotten. I could use them here. *Feeder hose, valve handle, wax gasket, a new toilet, porcelain patch and some floor prep.*

Looking up from the floor, my eyes locked on the wall space previously hidden by the tank. Four different colors stared back at me from the 4-square-foot area. *Guess I'll have to paint that. Feeder hose, valve handle, wax gasket, new toilet, porcelain patch, floor prep, white paint and one medium paintbrush.*

At the hardware store, I found everything I needed. They even gave me a free wax gasket with the new toilet I purchased.

Unfortunately, since the old linoleum had deep grooves, I had to fill in all the lines with a thin grout that the hardware store employees were oh-too-happy to sell me. Of course that also required me to buy some additional tools.

Back at the house, I swung into action. Clean the wall, clean the floor, paint the wall, grout the floor and wait, wait, wait for the grout to dry. I wanted to finish the job before Bonne came home and I impatiently watched the dark, gray goo dry to a light gray solid. Laying the tile was easy. The hardest part was peeling the paper off the back in one piece, which was something I never really got the hang of. Every time I'd pull, the paper would tear unevenly and leave me picking at the stray stuck-down ends with my well-chewed fingernails.

Finally, it was done. The molding was back in place. Our fixed toilet stood, proud and sparkling, in front of a freshly painted wall. The wood-grained tile looked perfect and professional. Now all I had to do, while I waited for my wife to arrive, was come up with a good explanation of how a $1 job turned into a $250 dent in our bank account!

*Hmmm*, I mused to myself. *I wonder if I Bonne's ever heard of the Domino Effect?*

# The Powderless Powder Room

by
David Martin

We recently renovated the bathroom in our nearly 50-year-old home. At the same time, we had a new half-bath built in the basement. My wife and daughter are thrilled with the renovated bathroom. I, too, have to admit that it's a pretty spiffy biffy. And I have reserved my greatest delight for the new half-bathroom. For this new room, small as it is, belongs to me.

It's been said that a man's home is his castle. I don't know who said that, or when, but I suspect it was many years ago when people actually lived in castles. Today, it's more accurate to say that a woman's home is her castle. Most men have yielded to women when it comes to home management. Let's face it—it's the rare fellow who involves himself in choosing floor patterns, carpet colors or the mysteriously named window treatments.

That doesn't mean we men can't still have a throne, which brings me back to our new half-bath or, to be more precise, *my* half-bath.

I let my wife have free reign when it came to the do-over of the upstairs bathroom. But the trade-off was that I got to choose what went in the new half-bath. Cheryl spent countless, joy-filled hours visiting every home improvement, tile and plumbing fixture store in the city for the upstairs bathroom. I, on the other hand, did not agonize over any of the choices made for our new mini-bathroom.

The tiles? The first serviceable, beige-colored ones I saw.

The vanity? The cheapest white, two-drawer one I could find on the Home Depot website.

The mirror? The $50, no-frame, easily attachable one that happened to be on sale.

The toilet? The budget biffy at Home Depot in the higher-than-standard height that will allow me to arise from it well into my 70s.

Short, sweet and simple. That's my secret to a successful renovation. My new half-bath may not make it into Better Homes and Gardens—hell, it may not even make it into Adequate Homes and Gardens—but it's everything I ever wanted in a powderless powder room.

No longer must I battle with my wife and daughter for private time in the upstairs john. Now there is one room reserved just for me. I don't care that it's small. I don't care that it's a bit cramped. I don't even care that there's no shower. It's a room with a sink, a seat and a door. Who could ask for more?

Each morning, I descend to my private cave where I can take as long as I want to shave, brush my teeth or just sit. No one is knocking on the door, urging me to hurry up or complaining about noxious fumes. I now have my own hideaway, my own meditation chamber, my own reading room.

I didn't anticipate how much I would enjoy, cherish and jealously guard my new private retreat. Sure, in an emergency others are permitted to use the half-bathroom, but on the understanding that any such visits must be temporary and brief. Under no circumstances is such a visitor permitted to leave any of her makeup, toiletry or grooming items behind. I have worked hard to achieve a Spartan decor and I will fight to the death to maintain it.

In my experience, if you allow one or two fancy soaps or shampoos in a bathroom, they breed and multiply until they populate every ledge, counter and empty space. And if your guard is down and such insidious items as dried flowers, wall hangings and incense sticks make it past the door, the battle for one's own men's room is all but lost.

I have additional rules for my bathroom. Much like Martin Luther once nailed his 95 Theses to the door of the Castle Church in Wittenberg, Germany, I intend to post my bathroom guidelines which might read something like this:

- No colored bottles, knickknacks or shiny rocks on top of the toilet tank.
- No fluffy covering on the toilet lid.
- Absolutely no toilet roll cozies allowed.
- Reading material consists solely of one book and one magazine of my choice.
- Occasional visitors may temporarily bring in personal reading matter, but any women's or teen magazines

left behind will be unceremoniously disposed of as I see fit.

- No cute curtains on the small basement window.
- No single wall hook holding a fancy embroidered hand towel unintended for actual use.
- No fancy soap dish in the shape of a fish, turtle or frog.
- No seashells on the counter, floor or window ledge.
- Absolutely nothing scented, especially talcs, lotions and powders.

I have taken to my new room like a teller to a bank vault. I guard my half-bath and ensure that it retains the security and simplicity that I have come to cherish.

As the years pass, I am sure that I will be able to maintain my new Fortress Dave as a bulwark against the outside world which is primarily populated by my wife, my daughter and our dog.

I don't wish to appear rigid or mean in my approach. While I may seem strict in applying certain standards, I am open to future changes to my room.

For example, I am not averse to installing a small TV so that those viewing sporting events in the nearby rec room will not miss any of the action. And, space permitting, I would not entirely rule out the addition of a mini beer fridge.

But apart from these minor improvements, I see no reason to make any other changes. I am prepared to take a stand and defend my room to ensure that it remains for all time a potpourri-free zone.

Dave's perfect half-bath

# The Missing Gene

by
## Meg Mardis

My family knew the value of a dollar, and never spent a single one on a professional for home improvement. We weren't the only ones. Up and down the block, everyone was a charter member of the Sweat Equity club. The club insignia was crossed crutches and cuss words on a field of mercurochrome.

From painting to roofing, upholstery to rewiring, building tree houses to garages, there were always neighbors to lean on who had enough know-how and bravado to tackle any job.

Most opportunities to learn new skills were born of necessity and came out of the blue. My six-year-old brother, always an industrious soul, created an opportunity to remodel the kitchen. His job was to empty the kitchen wastebasket into the backyard wire bin for my older brother to burn. It was a time-consuming process that could prove dangerous. First he had to struggle into his snowsuit, boots, hat, scarf and mittens. Even worse, stepping outside made him a target for a barrage of slush balls launched by bullies down the block. Crouched snickering in their snow forts, they ambushed little kids who had their hands full and couldn't return fire.

With just minutes to go before the Flintstones came on TV, Arch decided to streamline the process. He lit the papers in the kitchen wastebasket. Voila! Scorched linoleum and melted shellac on the cabinets.

That January weekend dad learned to install linoleum, and mom discovered she had a knack for refinishing kitchen cabinets.

As for me, I might have learned more repair tips had I not been so busy building my vocabulary. Arriving at school most Mondays with a new crop of cuss words harvested while spying on dad, I shocked and dazzled the recess crowd. My popularity knew no bounds.

Two decades later when I finally met Ted, I never thought to inquire about his honey-do credentials. Love isn't just blind, it struck me dumb. Or maybe it was penance for eavesdropping when I should have been helping with weekend projects.

In my own defense, let me state outright that I assumed DIY genes were just that—part of the Y chromosome that all men get at birth. If women are from Macy's, surely men are from Home Depot.

My illusions were shattered one Friday a couple of months after our wedding when I was baby-sitting Amanda. I called to notify Ted of the crisis just minutes before his afternoon meeting.

"Precious," I said, "the downstairs toilet is stopped up."

"How can that be? The house isn't old enough to have bad plumbing."

"Well, Amanda's here and she flushed a hand towel."

"Who's Amanda?"

"My niece! She was the flower girl at our wedding, remember? She wore a white organza pinafore and carried a basket of tea-rose petals."

"Is she the one that bit me at the reception?"

"Yes, precious. She didn't mean it, she was still teething."

"She grabbed my finger, leaned forward and bit me. And why is she flushing hand towels anyway?"

"I don't know, I guess two-year-olds flush things."

"Well that's just wrong. You ought to have a talk with your brother."

"Yes, dear. So can you fix the toilet when you get home?"

"Sure, no problem, my pumpkin. Just don't let Vampira flush anything down the other toilet."

"Her name is Amanda, and I won't. Thank you, precious, you're my hero."

Arriving home just after seven o'clock, my beloved sprang into action. "There's nothing quite as handy as a man around the house," I hummed.

"Precious, can I get you any tools?"

"No need," said my prince. "I've got the phone book right here."

"Why do you need the phone book?"

"To get the number for Roto-Rooter."

"Aren't you going to fix it yourself, Ted?"

"Ick," he said.

"My dad and brothers never call a plumber."

"Well then you should have called one of them."

"Wait! You could call my dad and he could talk you through it."

"I don't want to know even the first thing about fixing a toilet."

"But you said you'd take care of the toilet when you got home."

"I am taking care of it," he said dialing the phone.

"But you're just calling a plumber. I could have called a plumber!"

"Yeah, I was wondering why you didn't. It's the weekend now, and they'll charge double time."

Call Roto-Rooter, that's the name. And away goes illusion down the drain.

# Finally Flush

by
## Maureen Rogers

Years ago, my husband courageously strapped on a tool belt and started swinging a hammer. His first project was our 750-square foot, two-bedroom, one-bath home. We lived with open stud walls and sawdust for nearly two years and he was still pounding in the final nails the day we sold the place.

To this day, he groans if I mention the bathroom remodel in that house. A friend had shown him the basics of plumbing, wiring, drywalling and tiling and he was a fast learner. But his budding "I-can-fix-anything" attitude nearly derailed permanently on that job.

Confident after the sink and tub installation, he announced we would soon have a toilet again. It was an exciting moment in our little household. No longer would we have to run to the gas station on the corner or use our 5-gallon drywall bucket during the night. Who knew affixing the toilet to the floor was as simple as attaching an inexpensive wax ring and screwing in two bolts at the base of the toilet bowl? Amazingly, gravity held everything in place and in less than 30 minutes, we were flush.

While the plumbing appeared to work, a few hours later a puddle appeared behind our new toilet. My husband poked and prodded and finally determined, just minutes after the hardware store closed, that the seal was the problem. "Sorry, honey. Better get out the bucket again tonight."

The next morning, he returned from the store with a new wax ring. He checked with the clerk and was confident he'd followed the instructions correctly. Not long after the second installation, I heard a moan come from the bathroom. This time, the puddle behind the toilet was the size of a small pond.

I made a joke about heading to the basement for his fishing hip waders, but he didn't laugh. I broached the next comment more delicately. "Maybe we should call a plumber, dear."

The image of a man on his knees gripping a wrench and glaring back from toilet-bowl height has been imprinted on my brain ever since. I slipped silently from the room and waited out the day, with trips to the gas station when needed. Meanwhile, he manned the barricades, filled the sandbags and continually replaced towels around our new commode.

The next morning, my handyman husband woke up to a light-bulb moment—the hardware store must be selling defective wax rings! Two hours later, he returned with a selection from a larger chain store across town.

But the gusher continued.

He turned red and the air turned blue in our tiny bathroom. I peeked in after a while. "Maybe we should think about that plumber now," I suggested.

The slow burn of silence followed and for the sake of our marriage, I retreated once again. Soon after that, I heard him on the phone to the hardware store manager, ending the call with, "OK, I'll give it one more shot."

An hour later, I found him slumped over the toilet bowl—in a pool of water—a broken man. "Get the phone book. We need a plumber."

I returned with the *Yellow Pages*, just as he was pulling the toilet up to scrape off the waxy buildup. That's when I saw something. I squinted and took a closer look. "What's that?" I said, pointing to the toilet.

"What?" he looked to where I was pointing—a hairline crack ran across the underside of the toilet base. "Holy expletive!" was all he said. It wasn't the seal after all. The toilet was defective.

Despite the trauma, my husband claims the experience was a confidence builder. It's not always the do-it-yourselfer who's to blame when things go wrong. He's proven his skills many times over and we've never had to bring out the drywall-bucket potty again. Our current home, which originally had two toilets, now has five. And to this day, my husband still denies that excessive toilet number has anything to do with a lesson too well learned.

Husband Don

# Deep Doo Doo

by
### Terri Duncan

The first Christmas in a new home is supposed to be a memorable occasion, and ours certainly was. However, it was memorable for a far less Christmassy reason than I would have chosen had I had any say so in the matter. Just a couple of hours before my husband's entire family was due to arrive at our house for the annual holiday feast, my young son's voice rang out through the house.

"Momma! Come quick! The downstairs potty is making funny noises!"

My little boy is something of an alarmist, so I initially ignored his frantic cry. My husband was in the shower. I had a ham to baste and potatoes to mash. And at some point, I still had to drag myself away from the stove to get dressed in festive attire. A flushing toilet was of little concern to me at that particular moment.

In retrospect, I should have responded to my little boy's call. Perhaps if I had done so, I would have discovered rising waters in the toilet bowl, accompanied by gurgling and bubbling. It was only when my daughter called out, "Momma, is water supposed to come out of the potty?!" that I responded appropriately and came running.

Entering the downstairs bathroom, I was greeted by a toilet-sized version of Niagara Falls. My screams brought my towel-clad, dripping husband clamoring downstairs. While he scrambled to turn off the valve, my children and I rushed upstairs to gather towels to sop up the mess that now trickled out of the bathroom and into the hallway.

Our guests would be ringing the doorbell at any moment, the ham was drying out in the oven and I just knew that unspeakable bacteria were contaminating my children, as well as my husband and me. My maniacal tears were only adding to the rising water level. While we frantically mopped, wiped and sanitized, the children escaped the lunacy and went to the playroom to make an "Out of Order" sign. We barely had time to mount it on the bathroom door before our guests began arriving.

The next day—Christmas Eve—brought all sorts of merriment to our address. The plumber, who made a special visit that day, informed us that all was well with our pipes, but we should have our septic tank pumped. He was full of joy when I handed him an exorbitant check for his holiday services.

"Merry Christmas!" he shouted, as his truck rolled out of sight.

"Bah! Humbug!" I muttered, slamming the front door

and sending the Christmas wreath flying.

The septic tank pumper guy was just as joyous, despite the fact that he was ankle-deep in matter that most certainly did not emit the aroma of evergreen and holly. His jolly grin and "Happy holidays!" could obviously be attributed to a hefty holiday payment courtesy of one of Santa's not-so-happy elves.

Bah, humbug to him, too, I thought. I certainly hoped he was going to have a merry damn Christmas. I was not! My Christmas spirit had long since gone down the toilet. At least something had!

More toilet catastrophes helped us ring in the New Year and our already meager after-Christmas checking account balance was dwindling at a dangerous pace. Perhaps that was the impetus for my husband, an avid do-it-yourselfer, to assume the role of plumber, pumper and septic system re-doer.

"You know," he said one day after perusing the Internet in search of information on septic system repair, "I think I've got this thing figured out!" He went on to describe this elaborate plan for repairing what was obviously a septic system that had not been installed in the most optimal manner. I nodded my head in agreement and graciously commented on his intricate drawings.

"I think you're right," I said when he finally tossed his now-dull pencil aside. "So, who can we hire to get this done?" I was so ready to utilize water throughout the house without having to first assign one of the children to potty-listening duty. At the first sign of a bubble, belch or gurgle, all water usage in the house ceased immediately.

My husband looked at me as if I had just asked the most

ridiculous question conceivable. "Hell no, I'm not hiring anybody! I've already put out enough cash to experts, and they haven't managed to fix shit! This time, I'm handling things."

Now, without question, my husband is an intelligent, talented man. I did not doubt that he could do the job. I could not fathom why such a seemingly smart man would choose to handle such a repulsive task just to save a few dollars.

"Honey," I said, choosing my words carefully. I didn't want to injure his ego in any way. "Are you sure that you want to take this on by yourself? It just seems so gross to me."

My intelligent, talented husband, however, did not heed my sage advice and chose instead to dig around in that which may appear to be wholesome, rich earth. Not!

Days later, with all of his supplies in the yard, he went to work. When I checked on his progress after an hour or so, I was forbidden to come close to the work area.

"Don't come out here!" he shouted when I approached. "I don't want you near this crap!" I, too, am somewhat intelligent. Thus, I didn't have to be given the command more than once. And I didn't mind being relegated to the confines of my home's warm, sweet-smelling surroundings while he voluntarily traipsed about in the unmentionable.

Some time later, I heard a knock at the backdoor. I opened it and there stood my shivering, dirt-smeared husband, clad only in a pair of boxer shorts.

"Where are your clothes?" I asked, reaching for something with which to cover him.

"Trash can," was his weak response.

"And where are your boots?" I asked, trying desperately

not to turn away from the odor now emanating from his near-naked body.

"Left 'em in the woods," he answered, taking the towel I held out to him. "I think I'll go take a shower now," he mumbled, stepping gingerly into the house, trying to come in contact with as few surfaces as possible. "It might take a while."

Since that day, our plumbing problems have ceased. We have had no overflowing toilets or tanks. My do-it-yourselfer husband decided he would never again tackle any job dealing with septic systems or human excrement. And, my smart and intelligent husband decided unequivocally that no price is too high to pay when it comes to dealing with shit.

What about the rubber boots he left standing in the woods? All these years later, they remain in the precise location in which he left them, a reminder to us all.

The toilet and the boots

# CHAPTER FIVE

# Martha Stewart Doesn't Live Here

---

But I wish she did!

---

# Reverse-Engineering

By
## Monica Giglio

When spring arrived, I decided to enhance my outdoor living space with curtains I made from Sunbrella fabric. For those of you not in the know, Sunbrella fabric is the leading name in outdoor, weather-resistant, mildew-free fabrics for awnings, patio furniture and outdoor draperies. And just like "Kleenex," for many of us, the name "Sunbrella" is a generic way to include any and all types of outdoor fabrics.

The outdoor living space I was creating was situated on a covered porch. I enclosed a portion of my deck with a real roof with shingles and everything. Under it, I placed an L-shaped outdoor sectional, a rug and a TV. Outdoor draperies in a trendy color and pattern were all that was still needed to finish my new project.

After fabricating the drapery panels, I decided to mount them on a board with a staple gun rather than hang them on curtain rods. In my collection of assorted tools, I located not one, but two staples guns. One was standard and the other was a desktop stapler that converted to a staple gun.

Moments of frustration quickly followed when I realized both guns were nearly empty. Not one to give up easily, I scrounged around and found some partial sleeves of staples and got to work, hoping they would last to the end of the project. I was nearly finished when I abruptly ran out of staples in the second gun—the first had run out earlier. Up on the ladder, with both arms over my head, one pinching pleats and holding the drapery panel in place and the other, holding the staple gun, I wasn't happy. "You gotta be kidding me!" I said to no one in particular.

I was pissed, but I wasn't ready to give up. Coming down off the ladder, I dropped to my hands and knees and resorted to delicately inserting stray single staples that had scattered when I had accidently dropped some partial sleeves earlier. I would get one or two into the tray upright, but every time I had a third or fourth one inserted, they all tipped over and turned sideways! "You suck, you little bastards! Why won't you cooperate?!" I yelled to the inanimate staples refusing to stand up in the tray.

It became painfully obvious that my idea wasn't going to work, so I hopped into my Jeep and headed for the store we all know as Staples. It seemed like the obvious choice as I walked in toting a staple gun in each hand, evoking images of Annie Oakley. The store clerk was very helpful, but doubtful he would have what I needed.

"Really? Not even for my convertible desktop stapler? But we're in Staples, aren't we?" I asked with a friendly smile.

He took me to a tiny section at the end of aisle four. Together, we sifted through the few varieties of little boxes of staples they had. *Specific staples for specific guns?* Why can't they be universal? I thought to myself as we squatted near the bottom row.

The Staples employee was slightly embarrassed as he searched. "No, this won't work. Wait, maybe this one," he mumbled through a half smile. He considered box after box then returned each one to its little spot on the little shelf in the little area designated for little staples at Staples.

Finally, he said, "I'm sorry, ma'am. I think maybe you should try Home Depot."

Home Depot? Really? That big, huge, gigantic store for a little box of staples? Luckily it was right around the corner, and although daylight was fading, I held on to the hope that I could finish my project before nightfall.

At Home Depot, I found another pleasant employee and asked her if she could help me find the right staples for at least one of my guns.

"This is what you need," she said, handing me a box of quarter-inch T19 staples. "See? Quarter inch, just like it says on the side of your staple gun." I thanked her. But on the way to the register, I decided to double-check the fit—and I couldn't get them into the gun!

I spotted a tall, burly, young employee. "Can you show me how to load this thing?" I asked, feeling a bit incompetent, but appealing to his machismo at the same time. When he couldn't load it either, I breathed a sigh of relief.

He declared, "These aren't the right staples for this gun. See?" He pointed to the side of the staple gun. "Yeah, these are quarter-inch, but it says here you need T20s or T25s."

Back to the staple aisle we went. He laughed when I told

him I had originally gone to Staples for staples; the irony wasn't lost on him. As he picked up box after tiny box, it became painfully obvious that I was not going to be able to get the specific staples required for either of my guns. But before giving up and going home discouraged, I had an idea.

"Why don't we reverse-engineer this problem?" I offered. "Looks like you have plenty of T50 staples here. Do you sell a staple gun that takes T50s? Maybe I need to buy a third staple gun and a lifetime supply of staples to go with it."

He laughed again and helped me find a staple gun that took T50s. He even unpackaged it and showed me how to load it. I left the store feeling a bit excessive, carrying three staple guns and more T50 staples than I would probably ever need in my lifetime. I wasn't going to go through this again!

As I hoped, I was able to hang the panels before nightfall and another home improvement project was complete, thanks to a helpful employee and some creative reverse-engineering.

Monica's outdoor space

# Peach Pits, Grits and Hissy Fits

by
Cappy Hall Rearick

Everything I needed to know about home decorating, I learned from Heloise. She taught me how to rearrange heavy furniture without throwing my back out and how to cover up detracting features on my walls by hanging large pictures over the top. And the great Heloise showed me how to decorate doorknobs with white spray paint and decals.

What is more amazing is that the woman advocated the reuse of items long before "repurpose" became a household word:

"Make curtains for your basement windows from old shower curtains."

"Use an ironing board for a bedside table. Plenty of room for books, lamps, radio . . . even the iron in case the spirit moves you in the middle of the night."

"Put a chest of drawers inside your closet then clutter the top of it to your heart's content. Nobody will see the clutter but you."

Is it any wonder that Heloise became my home décor guru? Not only did she teach me how to cut corners to make my life flow more gently down the stream, she showed me how to make a beautiful dining area with a simple card table covered with an old shower curtain. And I learned how to refresh my plastic flower arrangements by dipping those puppies in food coloring.

She was a genius, the Dr. Oz of housewifery, the self-anointed Housewife Heroine.

My best friend Paula scoffed at my allegiance to Heloise. Openly smirking, she would recite passages from Peg Bracken's *I Hate to Housekeep Book* and order me to listen up. Peg was Paula's kind of woman.

Even so, I remained loyal to Heloise no matter how often Paula dissed her. To my way of thinking, a woman's home was a reflection of her soul. I adhered to Heloise's hints on cooking, decorating and boundless other ways of life made simple.

With each new kitchen hint, I would morph into a human Secretariat, snorting and stomping at the gate while foam gathered around the spoon bit in my mouth. Her decorating ideas sent me racing to Ace Hardware or to the nearest Walmart, depending on my monthly budget.

"When Heloise taps into your brain cells with another of her crazy ideas, you act like you just discovered the multiple orgasms," Paula said. "You seriously need to get a life."

I responded by reaching across the kitchen table to brush s'more crumbs from the front of her coffee-stained T-shirt.

She sighed. "Or not."

My Heloise focus kept me out of stores and boutiques and for that, my husband, Babe, was grateful. The man was the next thing to Gandhi each morning while I read, as if quoting scripture, Heloise's hint of the day. I'd open one of Heloise's books at random and allow my finger to fall willy-nilly on the page. Those words under my finger then became the universal message of the day. My devotion, akin to that of a Trappist monk, grew in direct proportion with each message I received.

"Save those peach pits," the Kitchen Queen proclaimed one morning. "When placed under pillows, your guests will thank you for sweet-smelling dreams."

I thought I had hit the jackpot, the loving cup—the mother lode of mother lodes. I dashed to the Piggly Wiggly, bought three bushel baskets of peaches and went peach-pit crazy. What my family didn't eat, I froze, of course according to Heloise's chapter on freezing fruit for eternity and beyond. Ten years later, we drank spiked punch at one of my weddings, fermented from those same peaches. It was darn good, too.

I could hardly wait to tell Paula.

"I put more than 100 peach pits under my guest room pillows."

Paula said, "Tell me the truth. How many cups of laced coffee are you drinking these days?"

"Don't be silly, Paula. I drink two cups of decaf and you know it."

"OK, then give me one good reason *not* to think that you're rolling down the highway at mach speed in the direction of Squirrel City."

"Heloise says that peach pits can freshen as many as 100 pillows."

Paula rolled her eyes. "Yeah, yeah. And remove plantar warts and nose hair, too. Uh, Cappy, need I remind you that you don't own 100 pillows?"

As if I were about to impart the meaning of life, I leaned toward her, my eyes dancing like Peter Pan on crack. "It never hurts to be prepared."

Months later, my peach pits were lounging totally forgotten under the guest room pillows, abandoned that is, until Babe's former boss showed up with his wife for a weekend visit.

Babe wined the couple and I dined them. He bought chardonnay in a bottle instead of a box, I cooked Southern recipes and even shamed them into eating grits.

After dinner, the boss's wife yawned. Claiming jet lag, she opted to go to bed early.

As soon as she got upstairs, she turned down the covers. When she picked up a pillow to fluff, however, a nest of forgotten peach pits stared up at her as if they had eyes.

She was from somewhere north of the Mason-Dixon Line, and immediately assumed that the things sleeping under her pillow were Southern cockroaches, along with all of their descendants.

She freaked.

We ran upstairs as soon as we heard the screams. By the time we got there, she lay huddled in a fetal position in the far corner of the room. I could be wrong, but I could have sworn she was sucking her thumb.

When they came downstairs the next morning, they said

something had come up and that they would be leaving right after breakfast.

I wrote a nasty letter to Heloise blaming her harebrained peach pit idea for the entire debacle, as well as Babe's severed connection from his former boss. I didn't mention my need for long-term intervention.

Heloise, ever gracious, replied. "Sometimes life is the pits, Toots. Get over it."

# Pinterest
# Made Me Do It

by
### Abigail Green

Like a lot of people I know, I have a love/hate relationship with the website Pinterest. On the one hand, I love looking at the pinboards people have created to showcase delectable recipes, funny quotes and gorgeously designed rooms.

However, if you're not careful, Pinterest can send you into a delusional DIY tizzy. Before you know it, you're thinking to yourself, *I could totally do that. I could whip up a funky, modern coffee table out of reclaimed wood and tricycle parts in a single afternoon. Bring on the power tools!*

That was me. I wanted to try everything, even a big project that required power tools. Never mind that my most ambitious home improvement project to date was sticking decals on my kid's wall.

When my oldest son was in first grade, I decided he needed a real desk. He had fashioned himself one from a toy workbench, which was both ingenious and a little pathetic. This was especially true when he tried to do his homework hunched over his rickety plastic faux desk while he was perched on an overturned crate. So I started looking around for a better solution. I suppose I could've just gone to IKEA or Target and bought him one, but because I am so eco-conscious (and/or cheap), I decided I wanted to find an old desk and fix it up.

While out walking one day, I happened upon the perfect desk at a yard sale—a kid-size desk with a ton of storage. The top opened up and there were bookcases on each side. It was covered in cobwebs and hideous chipped blue paint, but I could see past all that. I saw potential, and by potential, I mean I had seen what other people had done with old desks on Pinterest.

I tried to haggle with the old man who was selling the desk. He wasn't having it. Not only did I pay him the $40 asking price, but somehow I ended up giving him an additional $10 to deliver it to my door. Shrewd businessman, that yard-sale guy.

After taking my money, the man did, however, give me some free painting advice. In his expert opinion, he estimated it would take me a couple of weekends to knock out the project. *A couple of weekends?* I thought smugly. *No way. I'll finish it in a day.*

It turns out I was a little overconfident. I know some people can do yardwork while their kids play nearby. I know people who can cook and clean and actually accomplish things while their children are awake. I am not one of them. Case in point: I tried to sand the desk while my boys—ages three and a half and six—played in the backyard, but they were far too interested in the electric sander. They got closer and closer to it as I worked, attracted as they are to anything that makes noise and has a plug. "Back away from the cord!" I shouted, choking on the dust. Plus, lead-based paint particles probably aren't the best thing for kids' lungs, anyway.

Next, I tried to paint the desk while they played in the kiddie pool. I think I got half of one leg done before my three-year-old decided it would be a good idea to jump off the deck into the pool. It wasn't. He took a flying leap off the edge, splashed into the 6 inches of muddy water in the pool, and then landed squarely on his butt when his feet slid out from under him. I put down my paintbrush and went over to kiss his boo-boos.

Finally, it was decided that I would have to wait to work on the project until my husband could take the boys out for several hours. What was I thinking—several more hours? It took me two more entire days—and two more coats of paint—to finish that desk. If you add the hours it took to sand it, the total time for the entire project was four days, spread out over three weekends.

The results were worth it, though. The desk came out great and my son loves to do his homework on it. I even refinished a real chair to go with it. Now all I have to do is post a picture of my handiwork on Pinterest so I can lure some other poor sap into an "easy" weekend DIY project.

The real desk

# Chase to the Cut

by
## Lisa Tognola

"You didn't make the cut, but thanks for trying."

It was the story of my life, fruitlessly chasing my ambitions with Wile E. Coyote abandon. Somehow, I always fell short of capturing my prize. I was outwitted by the competition and left hanging in midair before falling into a chasm, howling in pain.

Later in life, I discovered all of my hard work and determination granted me distinctive and recognizable status in the form of obsessive-compulsive disorder. The disease allowed me to channel my formerly ineffective energy toward my greatest goal yet—home improvement.

Taking enormous pains to give my house a quality makeover, I spent two years selecting rare stone countertops and back splashes. I had beautiful handmade mosaic tiles imported from Turkey, and hired many contractors, including a French carpenter with a sexy accent.

Following renovation came the sterilization phase of the project. Armed with an arsenal of cleaning products, I scrubbed, scoured and Febrezed my way into every nook and cranny, eradicating my home of every possible germ left behind by the contractors.

My efforts to beautify my house paid off in more ways than one when my friend, Lucy, asked if I would place my home on the Ten Most Beautiful Homes Autumn House Tour sponsored by my son Henry's school. It was the first time my house would be on a home tour! I was elated and agreed. In my house-fixated state of mind, a house tour was a more important measure of success than winning a talent show, being part of a high school homecoming court and being given a major job promotion—combined. I had made the cut. This would be my opportunity to shine.

So what is a house tour? An event in which the entire community pays money to do what I did every day—debate whether grass cloth was the right choice for my office walls, scrutinize my sofa upholstery and wonder how my husband and I could afford all this.

I learned that preparing for the tour would be simple. Organizers would assign captains to man each house on event day. Captains would admit guests, ensure they removed their shoes upon entering, and then comment on some of the home's unique characteristics. In my house, for instance, they might discuss how our fixation on keeping things organic resulted in a sustainable and almost livable space. "The homeowners spared no expense in their effort to use natural materials throughout the house. For example, this exquisite custom bathroom sink is made from farmed Japanese bamboo, which retains its luster for a lifetime, as long as it doesn't get wet. The kitchen countertop is a Calcutta de' Oro marble quarried in Italy, chosen for its classic beauty and practicality. The homeowners have requested that it not be touched, as oily fingerprints could mar the surface. And the very delicate and fragile lights over the kitchen island are custom-designed, hand-blown glass lanterns. So as to not cause extra vibrations, please tread softly as you pass."

The homeowners' responsibility was to make their homes presentable, welcoming and festive. "Presentable" was a cinch for a person like me who gauges clutter according to whether the entire contents of the room could pass through the "12 items or less" express aisle at the grocery store. "Welcoming" could be achieved by simply taking down my front door sign which read, "For sanitary reasons, please do not enter."

Making my house "festive" would be my greatest challenge. It was November, and I was never the type to fill the house with pinecones and paper turkeys. My idea of autumn festivity is rallying my family to rake the backyard leaves. I do not, like some homeowners, decorate with intangible objects such as smell. Nowhere in my home will you find scented candles with delicious sounding names like "Cranberry Compote," "Pumpkin Medley" or "Turkey Surprise." These are the kinds of candles that, if lit all at once, gives off the essence of an entire Thanksgiving dinner. Preferring to keep things simple and organic, I keep a matchbook in the guest bathroom instead.

Unlike the other nine homeowners also chosen to place their

homes on the tour, who all scrambled to clear their houses of clutter, I had to add things to my home to give it that lived-in feel. Some would call my home austere. I call it soothing.

Some people fill their homes with family photos: "Here's Johnny and Sue. Here's Johnny and Brian. Here's Johnny, Sue and Brian." Why do I need to surround myself with photographs of my children? I already know who they are and I see them every day.

People seem to take comfort in owning knickknacks, like miniature spoons and Hummel figurines. I have never been an enthusiast of collecting cutlery for display, nor do I enjoy being under the constant watch of porcelain clowns.

I am content to accessorize my house with simple things that bring me joy, like my coffeemaker, paper-towel holder and toilet brush. My floors are devoid of debris and my countertops as barren as an old nun. Even my kids know not to linger in one space too long for fear of getting stashed in the mudroom closet along with their backpacks. That is, when I allow them visits home from their boarding school in Siberia.

Some people take delight in turning their refrigerators into expressive appliances by decorating them with magnets as if they were year-round Christmas trees. I rely on a calendar instead of refrigerator postings to remind myself to do things like bleach the bathroom grout, iron my underwear and have sex with my husband. I do not own an oinking alarm that sounds every time the fridge opens, warning me not to pig out.

I'm not much of a cook, but since it was a house tour with an emphasis on kitchens, I felt obligated to make it look like someone actually cooked in it. By the time I had finished staging my kitchen, it looked like an Ethan Allen showroom, right down to the artificial artichokes on each plate at the kitchen table. The gourmet vegetables represented the first course in our family's hypothetical expansive multi-course dining experience. The formal place settings, with cloth napkins and real Wedgewood plates, looked so convincing that even I was looking forward to the imaginary five-course meal that would replace our normal freeze-dried lasagna served on Dixie Disposables, with Crystal Light to wash it all down.

The house tour was a huge success and raised $17,000 for our school. The expected 350 headcount grew to 450 by the end of the four-hour tour. In germ terms, at an average of two plantar warts per person, that translated to approximately 700 warts that marched across my kitchen floor, which collectively grew to an epidemic 900 cases of potential foot fungi for the entire school district. But regardless of all the fungi in my home, I finally understood what it meant to give back to the community. Volunteering for a worthy cause helped me realize that success is about the process, not just about making the cut.

And yet still, a few months later, as my podiatrist scraped a relentless fungus from my right toe, I couldn't help but gloat to myself about how I had finally triumphed. Just at that moment, Dr. Healey took a firmer grip of my foot, looked up at me and said, "You also have a suspicious-looking mole here. I'm sorry, but I'm going to have to make a cut." Then he warned, "Brace yourself, it may be deep," the latter part which sounded uncannily like Road Runner's cry—"Beep! Beep!" The incision didn't hurt nearly as much as the familiar pain of defeat. I howled.

When I got home, I told my husband that I would have to take a series of medications and wrap my foot every night. I worried about how I would keep track of everything. "Don't worry," he assured me. "We'll organize it for you by making a chart. We'll just buy some magnets and post it on the refrigerator."

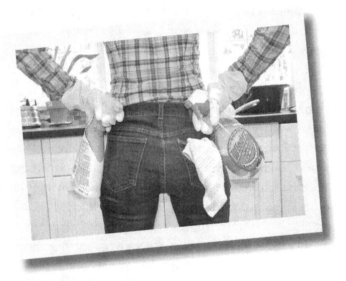

Lisa in cleaning mode

# An Uncontrollable Urge

by
Judi Tepe

Sometimes women just have to rearrange the furniture. It's part of our DNA. For me, this can only be accomplished when my husband goes fishing for the weekend.

As soon as I receive word of an impending trip, I begin to plan my new room arrangement. Patience is the key to a successful outcome. It's always difficult to restrain myself, but waiting 45 minutes until he's safely on the freeway is well worth the effort. Otherwise, without fail, he forgets something and returns just as I'm moving a chair.

Each time, my husband has a comment for my rearranging ways. "Why do you need to move the furniture? I like it just the way it is," is his typical refrain.

My husband's idea of decorating is a La-Z-Boy recliner next to a dorm-sized refrigerator, which also doubles as a side table. When it comes to accessories, the remote control is more than enough for him.

When I finally had the house to myself, my first order of business was to purchase fresh flowers and place them in my lovely crystal vase on the breakfast table. If I attempted to do this while my husband was home, within five minutes he'd have the sports section thrown over it. Inevitably, he'd knock it over then ask, "Why do we need flowers?"

All afternoon, I was busy moving sofas, chairs, end and coffee tables, lamps, magazine racks and pictures. I changed the throw pillows and transformed the character of the room. Then it became obvious that I needed a side chair for brightness and additional seating. I knew I couldn't spend too much money.

Pier One was having a sale, so I zipped over to take a look. I struck decorator gold when I found the most adorable floral chair, side table and matching lamp, all on sale. HGTV's Property Brothers have nothing on me. My husband would be pleased with all the money I saved.

On the way home, I stopped at my girlfriend's house. Her husband was with mine, so I was certain she was rearranging furniture, too. She loved the floral chair and had to have one. So off we went to Pier One. By the time we got back to her place, I noticed we were both having difficulty getting in and out of my van. Not a good sign.

I headed home for the cure and a change of clothes. After a handful of ibuprofen and a hot shower, I returned to my girlfriend's home, picked her up and we went to dinner. We both ordered steaks—for protein—and extra-large chocolate milkshakes, for energy, of course! We discussed the all-important next phase of all our home improvement projects—how to handle our returning husbands. Hopefully they had caught a lot of fish.

The next morning, I couldn't get out of bed. I was sure my back was broken. From a prone position, I called my partner-in-decorating-crime and found she was in similar straits. We agreed we'd have to wait for food until our husbands got home.

That evening, I was still in bed when I was startled by the crash of the fishing tackle box hitting the floor where only a short 24 hours ago, a table once stood. I was a little foggy from the Vicodin I had taken. The excruciating pain in my back was now shooting down my legs.

My husband appeared in the bedroom doorway and said, "You did again, didn't you?" He shook his head, knowing full well I couldn't move. He had been here and done that one too many times. I looked at him lovingly, anticipating his next question.

"Chicken noodle or cream of tomato?" he asked. "And where's my La-Z-Boy?"

# Let's Get Crafty

by
## Cindy Kloosterman

I like to think of myself as a crafty person. I love to knit, crochet, paint and make my own home interior decorations for the holidays. In fact, every year at Halloween, I make a wreath to put on my front door. Making a wreath is easy, and I'm going to share some crafting tips with you so you, too, can make your own Halloween wreath.

First of all, go to a store like Michaels or Hobby Lobby and find a wreath-shaped object. I usually buy a grapevine wreath because they're rustic and seem to fit in better with my fall theme. They're also cheap. Then gather some objects that fit in with your Halloween theme. I usually get fake silk leaves, fake pumpkins, fake berries and fake scarecrows to make my authentic Halloween wreath. I also buy ribbon, because for some reason I always forget that I cannot, no matter how hard I try, make a decent bow.

Once you get everything home, dump it out onto a table,

look at it for a few minutes, and then go get a really big glass of wine. Trust me, you're going to need it. This may also be a good time to treat yourself to a few pieces of Halloween candy, just to get into the mood. Chocolate and wine are good for you!

After you've eaten approximately six miniature Kit Kats, pick up your wreath and look to see if it's round. If it's not perfectly round, and most grapevine wreaths aren't, don't worry about it. You can always put a miniature fake pumpkin on the non-round side to balance it out.

I forgot to mention this earlier, but you're also going to need a hot glue gun for this project. WARNING: HOT GLUE GUNS ARE HOT!

Super Glue was my glue of choice for all of my projects, until I had an unfortunate accident about a year ago. I not only glued two of my fingers together, but also managed to glue my jeans to my stomach. It's a long story. So now I use a hot glue gun.

Plug in your hot glue gun. I live in an older house in the country and evidently the people that built my house didn't think electricity would really catch on. As a result, I have two outlets in each room, neither of which is convenient. I also own about 50 extension cords, but for some reason, I can only find one and it's too short. I move my table closer to the outlet.

After you've plugged in your hot glue gun, insert a hot glue stick into it and give the trigger a little squeeze to see if it's working. After you've done that, you'll need to either get a paper towel so you can get the hot glue off the table or get some

Bactine. That's in case, for some reason, you thought it would be a good idea to squeeze the glue onto your finger.

Refill your wineglass, eat several miniature Three Musketeer candy bars and place the hot glue gun on a glass plate. I've learned from experience if you put it on a paper plate, it will stick.

Take your ribbon and wrap it around your wreath. This may take a while because your hands may be a little shaky from all the sugar you've eaten. After you've wrapped half of your wreath, sit back for a few minutes and say some bad words because, if you're like me, you don't have enough ribbon. A few "dammits" usually makes me feel better.

Time for more shopping! If you've had less than two glasses of wine, grab your car keys and go back to the store where you bought your original ribbon. Walk to the exact spot where you found the ribbon yesterday. Then go find a clerk, because all the Halloween stuff has now been replaced with Christmas decorations. After you've gone to three other stores to find some Halloween ribbon, rethink your design and buy some non-Halloween ribbon that sort of matches. It's not like Martha Stewart is going to be trick-or-treating at your house, so you should be fine.

You'll probably want to pick up some more hot glue sticks since you probably left the gun plugged in and it's now oozed all of its glue onto your glass plate. It wouldn't be a bad idea to buy some more candy, either. Or wine.

Now that you're finished shopping it's time to get back to work! Pour another glass of wine. Remove the ribbon you originally wrapped around your wreath and spread it out a little. Glue the ends of the ribbon to the wreath. Re-glue them after you've pulled them off, because you wanted to see if they were actually sticking like they're supposed to. Depending on the amount of wine you've had, you may need to repeat this step a couple of times. Don't forget to open the new bag of chocolate bars.

Now it's time to put the silk leaves on the wreath. Open the bag of leaves. After you've picked them up off the floor, spread them out on your table and decide on your color scheme. Most silk leaves come in green, red and yellow. You can put them in any order, but you want them to look as random as possible. A few miniature bags of malted milk balls usually help me decide, so I suggest the same. My random order is usually one green leaf, one red leaf and one yellow leaf. Then I start back with the green leaf. I know, it sounds crazy, but it works for me.

After you've finished applying your leaves, it's time to sit back and admire your work. You may start thinking about how you could have bought a fully-decorated wreath for half of what this one is costing, but do you really want to be like everyone else? Of course you do, but that's beside the point.

Now for the fun part! First, go into your kitchen or craft room and open every drawer at least three times so you can find your wire cutters and scissors. Drink another glass of wine and think about it. Then go to your tool box and remove your wire cutters then go to your desk drawer and remove your scissors.

Pick up the wire stem that has all of your fake berries on it. Then pick up the phone and call your veterinarian because your bottomless pit of a dog has eaten all of them. After your vet assures you that these too shall pass, pick up your other decorations and glue them onto the wreath.

It's really beginning to take shape now, isn't it?

I mentioned before that I cannot make a perfect bow. However, I can make a reasonably acceptable one by using the following items: First you will need a *Monkees' Greatest Hits* CD case. You will also need a cassette-tape case, scissors, some wire, a paper towel and a Band-Aid.

Take some ribbon and wrap it around the CD case. Take some more ribbon and wrap it around the cassette tape case. Remove both and place the smaller ribbon on top of the larger CD-case ribbon. Now, take your scissors and cut a small notch on both sides of the ribbon.

Pick up your paper towel and wrap it around the finger you just cut with the scissors. You don't want to bleed on your ribbon. After the bleeding has slowed down, place the Band-Aid over the cut.

Sip your wine.

Now take your wire, insert it into each notch, turn the ribbon over and twist the wire. You may need to do this a couple of times because the ribbon always unwraps itself and you have to start over. After you've finally got the wire wrapped, fluff out the loops and hot glue the bow to your wreath.

Step back and look at your work, while again reminding yourself that Martha Stewart is not coming to your house this year.

*Voila!* You now have a personally handcrafted Halloween wreath for your door, and it only cost a little more than $100 and three days to make. Now ask your significant other to hang it on the door, because frankly, this artistic stuff will wear you out.

I hope my story has been helpful and will encourage you to try your hand at making your own decorations for your home. And I also hope you get lots of treats and no tricks this Halloween.

And that reminds me—I need to buy some more candy. And some more wine.

Cindy's $100 Halloween wreath

# Anyone Can Do It

By
## Tracy Winslow

"Anyone can do it!" they said. "It's so easy!" they exclaimed. "If you have a pulse, you can DO THIS!" Well I'm pretty sure I'm still breathing, although one glance in the mirror may discredit that belief. So I bought into the hype. I decided to get my craft on.

We had just closed on a new house and the girls wanted to paint their rooms. My six-year-old's furniture looks like it passed out after a termite rave. In the few years since we purchased Lena's big-girl bed set, she has colored and spilled on it with abandon. She has plastered it with stickers, glitter, nail polish and Bendaroos. Her awesome feats of gymnastics have sliced countless nicks into the set. A small family of fairies may have taken up residence in the bottom drawer. It was time for a furniture makeover to go with our new home.

I've never done anything like this before. So I researched the process extensively on Pinterest. After an hour of looking at hundreds of cute pictures, I was pretty much an expert. I went to the hardware store and impressed the clerk with my infinite knowledge of the process. "Um, I need some pinky colors and stuff to paint with, ya know?" I left armed with about $7,000 in paint paraphernalia and one tiny quart of paint called "Unrequited Love Pink."

When I got home, it was go time. I spread out the drop-cloth, which was actually a giant trash bag. I began with one of Lena's drawers. Because priming wood was for amateurs, I dove right in. One coat and I clearly saw that yes-anyone-can-do-this glow. And then the kids showed up.

"What are you doing with my stuff, Mommy?" Lena asked, eating a candy treat.

"I'm painting this for your new room. Isn't it pretty?"

Lena came over to investigate more closely. As she leaned over, she accidently poured her Texas-sized box of candy Nerds into the $20 quart of paint. "Oops," was all she said.

If you've ever painted with Nerds, you know this is not a task for novices. Thankfully, I had all that Pinteresting under my belt. So I mixed those little bastards right in and slogged through it. Unrequited Love Pink soon became Tainted Love, still pink but with a hint of Nerdy goodness. *I can do this. This is easy,* I kept telling myself.

All the commotion drew the attention of our two-year-old daughter Emmeline and our puppy, Loki. *Crap. Please be good, please be good.*

Realizing there was free Nerds candy to be had, Emmeline started fighting with Loki for the Nerds shrapnel on the ground, those stragglers that failed to make it into the can of expensive Benjamin Moore paint. Then the two turned their attention to the candy in the paint, both in the can and on the furniture. Lena joined in the fun. A flurry of motherly warnings ensued, but only a few I can actually list here:

"Don't eat that! There's paint on it!"

"Oh, my God! Get your face out of the paint can, Loki!"

"Stop touching the drawers! They're wet. No, you can't eat the chunks off the side of it!"

"Loki! Holy cow. DON'T LICK THE DRAWERS!"

"Yes, I know the drawers are bumpy. It's YOUR NERDS that you dropped in the paint! No, you can't pick them off!"

I found myself in prayer: Dear God, this was supposed to be easy. Maybe I don't actually have a pulse. No. I'm pretty sure I do, because the vein on my forehead is dancing the mambo.

Four hours, two pink kids and one pink dog later, only one measly set of drawers was painted. I looked at all the rest of the crap that I still needed to tackle and felt a little bit light-headed.

Back to Pinterest to research how to keep my kids and dog at bay. Wait! Hmm . . . what's this? It's so cute and would be so easy to do. How hard would it be to build a chicken coop?

The final pink drawers!

CHAPTER
SIX

# It Seemed Like a Good Idea . . .

---

. . . at the time!

---

# Free Labor, Anyone?

by
Pat Wahler

Adding a lovely iron wood-burning stove to our home seemed like a perfect idea. Our house was due to go on the market soon, and a stove would make an ordinary-looking living room much more appealing.

A bricklayer had already put down the hearth for us, but my husband, Phil, announced that he planned to vent the stove himself. I broke out in a cold sweat. It's not that he doesn't try, but Phil's home repair skills are not his most marketable asset.

It wasn't just me that noticed his lack of finesse. For years, our children witnessed their father's ingenious use of duct tape, accompanied by a torrent of curses, when fixing any item. They even coined a phrase for it. Hobbling a project together until a real repair could take place became, "Let's just 'Phil Wahler' it for now."

In a house of unfinished projects, agreeing to allow someone with such a reputation to cut a hole in the roof for a wood-burning stove sounded extraordinarily frightening, if not downright foolish. I decided to offer a more practical solution.

"That's a huge job. Don't you think we should let a professional do it?"

Phil snorted. "We don't need a professional. I have plenty of friends who can help. Then we won't have to pay for labor."

Phil's friends, many of whom are talented indeed, work cheap. Cases of beer and a pot of chili are considered more than ample compensation. This may sound like a good deal, until one considers that such a combination can bring outcomes that vary from wonderful to horrifying. Overruled by my well-meaning husband, Phil set the date and rounded up his buddies.

On the weekend of the project, I wrote a staggering check for materials, filled several coolers with beer and cooked an enormous pot of spicy chili. Morning birds were just beginning their busy song as his friends arrived. It didn't take long for the birds to flee the area as footsteps clomped from one side of our roof to the other.

The sounds of hammers and saws shattered the air. Each *boom, boom, boom* pounded home my fears. *Would someone amputate an arm? Crash through the ceiling? Tumble from the roof?* I worried to myself. Bits of wood, insulation and dust floated to the floor beneath the area where the stove would sit. The untidy pile grew at an alarming rate.

After my fourth inquiry into whether everything was going OK, Phil snarled at me to please go the hell somewhere else. By this time, my nerves were tattered enough that I agreed. I gathered my purse, bolted from the house and drove away. To keep from losing my mind, I created soothing mental images that featured a newly installed stove that looked like a picture from a magazine, perfect in every way.

I waited until just before sunset to go home. Dim lights always worked to make me look better, so I reasoned that this would surely do the same for my house.

As I pulled into the driveway, I noticed that the collection of cars in front had disappeared. No sounds of hammering, saws or shouts could be detected. Inside, I found Phil on the couch, snoring blissfully as the television blared. The newly installed stove sat in splendor on the brick hearth. Not even a shred of debris cluttered the top. I looked up at the ceiling. When I couldn't see sky, I figured that had to be a good sign. Perhaps I had misjudged my husband's talents.

The next morning, I got my first daylight look at the project. I had to admit, it looked professional enough. Phil strutted around the house like a triple gold-medal winner.

"All the ceiling needs now is a coat of paint," he informed me. His words held a hint of gloating, but that didn't bother me a bit. I heaved a sigh of relief.

Within a week, the appraisers would arrive to let us know how much money our house was worth. I deep cleaned every room while Phil touched up paint and problem spots. We needed to get as much money as possible for our place since we already had found a pricier house to buy.

On the day the appraisers pulled into our driveway, the house looked better than it had in years. I watched as two women dashed from the driveway to the door. I wondered why they were in such a hurry, until I heard a crack of thunder. The sky opened for the first drenching downpour we'd experienced in a month. The women came inside, shaking drops from their coats and umbrellas. They glanced admiringly toward the beautiful wood-burning stove. It was the perfect focal point to the room. Both of them smiled until all hell broke loose.

*Drip. Drip. Drip.* Moisture began seeping around the ceiling. First in small drops, and then water poured down the vent pipe and onto the stove, rolling off the hearth and spilling onto the floor in torrents. In no time at all, it appeared to rain as hard inside our house as out.

All three of us stared at the unintended water feature in horror. I did my best to explain. "I'm so sorry. My husband put this in just a week ago. It must need a little more caulk."

After uttering the understatement of the year, I grabbed a handful of towels and ran to the stove. Not having enough towels to contend with the mess, I finally gave up, allowing the pile of drenched towels to sit under the waterfall. I turned to the speechless women.

"Uh, would you like to see the rest of the house?"

In the end, the new wood-burning stove didn't add much value to our home. It did, however, give me a cost-saving lesson. No longer do I agree to "Phil Wahler" a project. Instead, I ask my son—who inherited his home repair skills from a different gene pool—or I hire a contractor.

My husband's a great guy, but the wood-burning stove fiasco proved something to me once and for all. Free labor really isn't what it's cracked up to be.

The Phil Wahler stove

# Stick-to-itiveness

by
### Beth Bartlett

We live in an old home, so gaps and breezes are part of life. But when our cats came and went as they pleased, even though we didn't have a pet door installed in the home, I became suspicious.

In the storage room, I found a space where a board had fallen away, revealing a large hole. In my mind, it became a cavernous entryway into our home, big enough for an armadillo pride parade, badger badminton team or two ninjas and a trained monkey.

I realized home repair was in order, but the hubby had a packed schedule. This left it up to me. That thought alone would make Bob Vila wake up with night terrors, mumbling, "Oh, my God, the duct tape . . . the DUCT TAPE!"

For me, hammers and nails were banned substances after a mishap involving hubby's thumb. I turned to alternate means of getting the job done. Duct tape didn't seem like the answer this time, so I settled on the seemingly innocent can of expanding foam. I've seen the hubby use it on numerous occasions and the foam always behaved itself. It rises nicely and turns rock-hard in minutes, just like my home-baked bread.

I read the instructions: "*Blah, blah, blah*, eye protection, shake can, hold can upside down for best results (*Kinky*, I thought, *But hey, whatever makes it stiff*) and always use gloves." Gloves? Ha! Gloves are for pussies. I didn't scream when a wolf spider ran across my foot last week, and he even tipped his hat and said, "Excuse me" afterward.

My strategy was to approach the hole from the outside and fill it top to bottom. I shook the can, slapped it a couple of times to keep it happy and hit the trigger. It belched, spit and squirted like it had eaten a week-old burrito from a truck stop.

The top layer flopped out of the hole and started a slow reach for solid ground, forming gloopy stalactites down the corner. It literally looked like the house had sneezed. I scooped it up with the end of the straw nozzle and shoved it back into the hole, but it was like trying to knit with melted circus peanuts.

As I fought the ooze back into the opening, I accidentally hit the trigger again just as I saw two eyes peeking out from the inside. At the exact same moment the nozzle sprayed, the cat hissed and I screamed, "Aaaaaaiiiiiiiiiiiigh!" Which is slang for, "Crap, now I have to shave the cat!"

The can also was startled, because the foam started spurting from the seal below the nozzle in a vain attempt to crawl up my arm and stop me. I dropped the can and ran back into the house to find the cat intact, un-foamed and under the couch.

On the bright side, I didn't have to go out and check the foam to see when it stopped being tacky. I knew the exact time it was no longer icky, because it was the same moment my fingers quit sticking together. When that happened, I was able to hold the scissors and cut the rest of the stuff out of my hair.

Tomorrow, I'm baking some bread and shoving that into the hole. It'll last longer.

# Rooftop Free-fall

by
## Dianna Graveman

I am afraid of heights. Standing on a tall chair can make me queasy. Climbing a ladder gives me vertigo. So when my father and my husband decided several years ago to install a new roof on our two-story home rather than call in professionals, I broke out in hives. Just listening to their heavy footfalls overhead was enough to send me to bed with a migraine.

A few summers later, the do-it-yourself duo decided they were going to paint the outside of the house. I stood on the front lawn clutching my chest as my husband, Don, leaned over the edge of the roof to reach the highest part of the house with his paintbrush. Dad, who was in his late 70s, acted as a human harness, holding tight to the back of Don's pants.

I needn't have worried.

"You know, Dad," Don called over his shoulder, loud enough for me to hear, "if something happens to me, your daughter and the grandkids move in with you!" Instantly, Dad began inching his son-in-law back from the edge.

Season after season, Don and my dad ignored my admonitions about broken bones and continued their rooftop repairs and high-ladder maintenance. At least a few times each season, my mother would inform me by phone that Dad was "on the roof again," cleaning out gutters or adjusting an antenna.

Then, on a mild January afternoon, my fear became reality. I had just returned home and was sitting in the kitchen when I heard a crash, followed by my husband's call for help.

Don had been standing on the top rung of a ladder, performing gutter duty, when the ladder shifted. Now he was sprawled out on the concrete driveway.

I grabbed the portable phone and ran to his side, dialing 9-1-1. "Don't try to move!" I instructed my husband.

"Don't worry," he said through gritted teeth.

I wasn't being sarcastic. Just a few months before, a friend's husband had fallen from his own roof and, despite intense pain, had immediately tried to stand. He blacked out from the agony of a broken back, smacked his head on the concrete and added a concussion to his injuries.

I was still trying to get off the phone with the dispatcher who seemed intent on learning my husband's life story and the details of every meal he'd eaten since kindergarten when an ambulance went careening past without stopping. Don had fallen between the house and a car parked in our driveway, apparently shielding us from view. Before I could get to my feet and out to the street to flag him down on the return, the driver sped past us the other way, lights flashing.

"Damn it!" I said as I ran into the middle of the street,

waving my arms wildly and jumping up and down. This time the driver made a U-turn and headed right for me, but I wasn't about to move—if he hit me, at least he'd have to stop.

One rough ambulance ride and several X-rays later, we learned Don had broken four vertebrae total, and one of them in two places. But he was going to be OK. Don spent a few weeks in the hospital and even more weeks at home, locked in a plastic body brace. If he followed orders exactly, the doctor said, he might be lucky enough to avoid surgery. He did, and he was.

Eight years later, our lives are pretty much the same as before the accident, except for one thing. Don threw away the ladder. He pays someone twice a year to clean our gutters. At Christmastime, lights twinkle from our doorway and shrubbery, but never from our rooftop.

Gone from Don's bucket list are items like parasailing and skydiving—doctor's orders forbid them. Gone, too, are roller coasters and horseback rides—also on the doctor's "no-no" list. But these missed recreational opportunities are a small price to pay for the ability to walk after a death-defying, rooftop free-fall. It took a near tragedy to get my husband off the roof for good, and he promises he will keep his feet on the ground where they belong and leave the aerial jobs to professionals from now on. I couldn't be happier.

Now, if I can only convince my 84-year-old father to stay off a ladder, too. I remind him of his weak knees, which give out now and then without warning.

"Oh, don't worry," he says. "They only give out at other times, never when I'm on the roof."

Well, that's a relief. Self-aware knees.

# The Formation of Death

by
## Kari Collins

I had just walked through the door when my husband, Bobby, immediately asked me, "Can you hear that beeping?"

"No." Then a second later, "Yes."

Noises don't bother me, having grown up in chaos. But all noises bother Bobby, with the exception of his Harley or *Gunsmoke* playing too loudly on the TV.

But this day, a beep was sounding every 10 seconds— the battery was going out in the smoke alarm in our bedroom. And every time it sounded, Bobby was 10 seconds closer to insanity.

Before I tell you what happened next, I have to say we are not handy people. We own very few tools because we recognize that in the wrong hands—namely, ours—we could commit accidental construction-related suicide.

The smoke alarm was located in a place where Columbus himself could not discover it unless Indians were living on it—on the bedroom ceiling, which is 16 feet high. I had never noticed it before because my eyes cannot see that far. I only found it because Bobby was now standing under it, with his arm straight up in the air, pointing out the offending item that would take a shuttle launch to repair.

After remembering that the ladder we owned was at his office, where we had done some minor remodeling, I suggested we call his brother and borrow his ladder. That, Bobby said, would not be necessary. "Why get a third party involved?" he asked. He then suggested I get on his shoulders and try to reach the smoke alarm. Having been kicked out of circus preparation class in college, I declined. Plus, I'm addicted to breathing.

So Bobby got a bar stool, instead. Climbing up onto it, he hit the smoke alarm with a crutch, causing the battery to pop out and land at my feet. But the alarm continued to beep! I suggested again that we call his brother. He acted like he didn't hear me and went running around the house, excited as a genius who just came up with the best invention since the ladder. But his invention made me wonder how he's lived this long.

Bobby carried a huge empty box into the house and mumbled something about how I wouldn't believe how strong a cardboard box really is. And he was right. I didn't believe it. Then he moved four bar stools into what I now call "the formation of death," laying the box across two of them, placing another one on top of the box and using the fourth one as a launch pad to the top chair. I don't know what the pillow was for—I nearly blacked out.

Bobby was on the first barstool when I started to say,

"You're not really going to . . ."

Then I said it. "Oh shit." This is my personal mantra in situations such as these.

My job was to hold the top chair steady, which is difficult when you're clutching your chest, but I managed. The entire time, Bobby was climbing to what I knew were his final seconds on earth. Trying to stay composed, I chanted to myself, Bad idea, Bobby. Bad idea, Bobby. Bad idea, Bobby, just like Dustin Hoffman in Rainman.

Believe it or not, Bobby actually got the battery changed. Then he looked at me afterward like, "Whaddya think I oughta do next?"

Reading his mind, I said, "Don't jump! That would be the second worst idea you've had today." Bobby got this look on his face he only gets when he thinks he's just had the best idea ever, something like an 11-year-old gets right before he jumps his bicycle off a ramp and over a 15-foot stretch of broken glass.

Without warning, he jumped. And he did the most beautiful tuck and roll I've ever personally witnessed. So good, in fact, that I forgot all about putting the orthopedic surgeon's number on speed dial in my phone in case another smoke alarm needed its battery changed.

I'm pretty sure Bobby lost an inch of his height during that death-defying stunt. He probably lost some feeling in his hips and maybe some range of motion in his ankles, too. When he woke up the next morning and dismounted the bed looking like a Transformer put together all wrong, he said, "I can't believe you let me do that."

Bobby's ladder

# News of the Day

by
## Linda O'Connell

We knew the 50-year-old fixer-upper needed a lot of work. But at least the price was right, the neighborhood was stable and the small starter home had possibilities. It was perfect for our family.

My husband and his buddy decided to remodel the kitchen. They acted like two kids at a carnival swinging the sledge hammer with all their might to see who was the strongest. If there had been a bell or buzzer to indicate the winner, they might have worked faster. Each time they made a dent in the wall, they sat down to admire their demolition work. If they hit a stud or took out a chunk, they hooted and hollered.

It took them nearly two months of working in the evenings to complete the job because they worked a while, sat a while and talked a while. They discussed the pros and cons of whether or not to close off a pantry. They tossed ideas out and asked my opinion on whether to angle or arch the doorway.

Should they relocate the sink? What did I know? I was just tired of doing dishes in the bathtub, and all I wanted was my oven to be operational by Thanksgiving. My stove stood in the center of the room like a giant chicken breast coated with plaster dust. I didn't think it would ever come clean.

Finally, I could see the light at the end of the tunnel. With the tile floor laid and the walls freshly painted, I could hardly wait to get shelves mounted and decorations hung. When the renovation was complete, I was quite proud of my new kitchen, with its spackled ceiling and new decor.

We then decided the exterior of the wooden framed back porch needed to be repainted. The porch, enclosed with storm windows, was just bigger than a walk-in closet, but it was the perfect snoozing place for our dog and cat.

My husband used a wire brush and scraper to remove decades of peeling paint from the porch. His hands were soon covered with blisters. Deciding to use a small hand-held propane torch to soften the paint and expedite the process, he was able to cover greater areas in shorter amounts of time, with less wear and tear on his hands.

While he was busy removing paint, I decided to lay wall-to-wall carpet in our 5-foot by 6-foot bathroom. I was a self-taught seamstress, and I knew how to lay out a pattern. I used newspaper and drew around the commode and sink. I carried the carpet into the living room. Then I flipped the carpet over and laid my paper pattern on top of the non-skid backing and began to cut with my scissors.

"Dad wants you to wait on that until he can help," my son informed me as I made the last snip.

"You just tell Dad to do his job and I'll do mine. I know exactly what I'm doing," I insisted. I had already purchased new accessories and didn't want to wait another day to complete the bathroom remodel.

I once again admired the dusty rose shade of the carpet as I anxiously hauled it back into the small bathroom and unfolded it. My eyes widened in horror and disbelief. The cut outs for the toilet and sink were on the opposite side of the room. How would I ever live this one down? Owning up to my mistake was all I could think of.

Slowly, I walked to the backdoor to admit my error. I heard the dog coughing and the cat yowling. I peeked out the window into the back porch area and noticed it filling with smoke. I yelled, "Fire!" and ran to the sink. I filled a dishpan with water and tossed it onto the porch just as my husband hopped off the ladder and entered. He gulped water, the dog gasped smoke and I ran for the phone.

The fire department arrived within two minutes, sirens blaring and red lights spinning. Our daughter and son ran to safety, each of them clutching an animal. Neighbors hovered on the sidewalk and watched as news crews and the Red Cross food van arrived. I was so embarrassed. The firefighters tromped through our house, dragging hoses and wielding axes. They ripped into the porch ceiling and walls. I nearly cried when they started toward the kitchen.

"Wait!" the captain shouted. "We've located the source."

He pulled smoldering newspaper from between the interior and exterior porch walls. They inserted the hose nozzle and soaked the walls while yanking out singed yellow newsprint.

"Years ago," he explained to us, "Some folks used newspaper as insulation in these old frame homes. We see this a lot."

As the emergency vehicles left, the cleanup began. "Might as well throw this bathroom carpet out and get a new one," I said.

"Why? The fire was on the back porch," my husband said.

"Oh, those firefighters, they tromped all over the place," I responded as I balled up the carpet and shoved wet newspapers on top of my botched job. To divert my husband's attention, I quickly changed the subject. "Why look at these headlines!" I said, picking up a sheet of yellowed newsprint. Then I read aloud the news of the day, circa 1957.

# It Hits the Fan

by
## Pamela Frost

I knew I'd spawned my new business partner when Chris was just two years old. I walked into his room and my son was standing there with all his plastic tools jammed into the waistband of his Underoos, "fixing" his toy box.

Twenty years later, Chris is my right-hand man. On one particular day, we were putting the finishing touches on our latest house-flipping project.

Chris was adding the last coat of paint on the kitchen cabinets. I was upstairs, trying to unclog the bathtub drain. For weeks I'd been dumping different brands of drain cleaner into it, with no results.

That morning, I resorted to sulfuric acid. At first, I poured the recommended 2 ounces into the drain and waited the recommended time. Nothing happened. I know sometimes the weight of water is enough to loosen a clog, so I put a few inches of hot water into the tub to speed things up. Nothing happened. I tried the plunger, but the water shot out the overflow. Again, nothing happened.

In spite of the directions on the bottle, I dumped the rest of the quart of drain cleaner into the standing water in the tub. It bubbled and spurted, putting up a visible cloud of rotten-egg fumes. Panicking, I knelt down and looked into the plumbing access hole to check the drainpipes—that's when I saw the acid seeping out of all the drainpipe joints.

Just then, Chris came lumbering up the stairs and into the bathroom. "Kitchen's all done, Mom. Wanna check it out?" Then he asked, "Ugh! Are you OK? What's that smell?"

I got up and put my hand on his chest, pushing him out into the hall as I coughed and gasped for air. "I'm using drain cleaner and the fumes are getting to me."

"You don't look so good, Mom. You'd better get something to drink and some fresh air."

We went downstairs and I sat on an upturned drywall bucket in the dining room. Chris fished an icy-cold ginger ale out of the cooler and handed it to me. I took a long and satisfying chug.

After I'd somewhat recovered, I went into the kitchen to admire his handiwork. Looking up, I noticed a slight bulge and a little yellow bubble on the ceiling. "Was it always like this?" I asked, pointing up and fearing his answer.

"Nope," Chris said, as he went to work touching up a few thin spots in the paint.

I sat my ginger ale down, grabbed some old towels and ran back upstairs. The sulfuric acid continued to bubble violently and seep out of all the pipe joints. I put the first towel down in the plumbing access hole under the bathtub. As I stuffed the second towel around the pipes, they came apart. The hot water and sulfuric acid gushed all over the bathroom floor and me then down into the hole that was the top side of the kitchen ceiling.

"Chris! Chris!" I yelled as I tried to shove the pipes back together. "Get me a bucket!" I was hysterical. I knew his beautiful paint job was about to be ruined. Worse yet, I had visions of the ceiling falling on his head.

Then I noticed my small Rubbermaid bin full of tools sitting nearby. I rushed to dump it out so I could catch the water, but it was too big to fit into the access hole.

That's when Chris came charging into the bathroom, breathless. "Big trouble Mom! There's water coming out of the kitchen ceiling!"

"I know, I know. I've been yelling for you."

I looked down as the last of the water trickled out of the tub. The damage was done. I went downstairs to inspect the mess. Chris, being a quick thinker, grabbed a kitchen drawer and sat it under the biggest stream of water in the center of the kitchen. I waded in, putting whatever was at hand under the smaller streams. I didn't know whether to cuss or cry.

Suddenly, my skin began to feel like it was on fire. I knew I needed lots of cold water to flush the acid off my skin, but the kitchen sink was under a dropcloth. Bolting to the basement, I opened the cold-water tap for the washing machine and rinsed my arms and legs.

Chris chased after me, concern clouding his face. "What's wrong?"

"The drain cleaner—it was sulfuric acid! I'm on fire!" I

said, hearing the panic in my own voice. Chris realized he, too, had a problem and got under the faucet beside me.

I went back upstairs to clean up the mess while Chris remained in the basement scrubbing frantically. Pulling the dropcloth off the sink, I wondered why it was so wet. Most of the water seemed to have come through the ceiling and around the ceiling fan in the center of the kitchen, but as I looked around, I noticed water dripping everywhere, even down the walls. I puzzled over this as I mopped the floor.

My skin caught fire again. I ran to the basement where Chris was under the faucet, now washing his hair. My arms and legs burned worse than before. I jumped in next to him, still confused over the drenched kitchen. "I don't understand it. Everything up there is wet!"

"That's because when the water started pouring out of the ceiling, the ceiling fan was on. Lucky it was on low."

"Lucky?" I looked at him, standing there dripping

wet in his boxers, and I knew I'd spawned an optimist. I was amazed that he found anything lucky about the day the acid hit the fan.

Chris and Pamela

# Burned Out

by
Suzanne Olsen

It was my husband's fault that I ended up in the doctor's office with my pants down and a crowd of interns looking at my bare ass.

My husband doesn't do projects around the house. His mantra is, "It's fine, just leave things the way they are, we'll do it later." I've started many projects simply because I'm too impatient to wait. Like the concrete project that landed me bottoms-up in the doc's office.

When we bought our 1954 fixer-upper, we hired people to tear out the Sheetrock, redo the wiring, bust up the concrete foundation to replace the old plumbing, and then put it all back together so we had a lovely, modern, spanking-new house. Almost.

They left one part undone. Workers had jackhammered a 3-foot by 7-foot hole through the concrete slab in the laundry room/storage area so we could turn part of it into a bathroom. When they were done, my husband put a piece of plywood over the hole and called it good.

"We've got to get that hole filled in!" I wailed, horrified that there was actually a hole in our floor with dirt and spiders and tree roots and worms and who knows what else, all of it just below that thin sheet of plywood.

"Nobody's going to see it," he said. "It's in the storage room. The plywood's fine. We'll do it later."

A couple of years of nagging didn't get me any closer to having that hole filled in, and I just knew that moles and other vermin had tunneled through the dirt and were breeding in that 4-inch space under the plywood. I didn't dare look. It gave me the heebie-jeevies every time I went in and out of the laundry room, which was several times a day.

Finally, I couldn't stand it anymore. While my husband was planning his annual boating trip with his friends, I studied books from the library, talked to concrete finishers then lined up a plumber to do the under-the-slab plumbing. And I went to Home Depot to buy supplies.

A half-hour after my husband walked out the door, the plumber arrived, roughed in a drain for the bathtub and toilet, and then left. I fed the kids and got them ready for bed.

Around 7 P.M., I rolled a wheelbarrow into the bathroom. I dumped the entire contents of a 60-pound bag of cement into the wheelbarrow and added water from a garden hose, which I had snaked into the house. I mixed the concrete and water with a shovel until it made a heavy, gray stew. I heaved the wheelbarrow up on end and poured the lumpy mess into the hole. It barely covered any of the dirt, but I didn't care. I was fixing that hole. Oh, what a wonderful feeling! Sheer ecstasy! I was drunk with joy.

However, I wasn't feeling so chipper at one o'clock in the

morning, 31 bags of concrete later. I'd finally filled the hole, but I couldn't get the surface smooth. It was full of lumps and undulations, and I knew that would be a nightmare when we got around to tiling the floor.

Exhausted, fighting off tears, my arms and back aching, I sat in the middle of the wet, semi-hard concrete and tried to even the floor. I raked the trowel back and forth, back and forth, back and forth. My bottom got wet from the cement then warm then hot! Still, I kept rhythmically sweeping the trowel like a zombie Frankenstein robot.

Finally, I threw in the trowel and gave up. It wasn't getting any smoother, and my bottom felt like I was sitting on two hot plates. I showered and collapsed into bed, careful to sleep on my stomach.

The next day, I woke up to searing pain and could barely walk. I called my doctor's office and after explaining the problem to the nurse, the doctor came on the line, intrigued. He told me to come to his office right away.

While I lay on the office exam table, bare bottomed and humiliated, a line of interns filed in, eager to see the show. How he rounded them up so quickly I don't know. The doctor told them what happened as the interns examined my second-degree chemical burns. It was so embarrassing—all four of my cheeks were red. The doc gave me a tetanus shot and heavy-duty painkillers. As I hobbled out the door, I could hear the interns' muffled laughter.

That night at my daughter's back-to-school function, I didn't dare sit down, but stood by the door and tried not to grimace. The teacher came over and pointed out a desk in the back of the room, asking me to sit. I explained that my buns were burning and it was too painful to sit, even with the painkillers.

When my husband came home a few days later, he was happy that I had filled the hole. He thought I'd done a good job, all things considered. Usually, he hates it when I do projects, especially without consulting him. This time, I think he believed the pain and humiliation were enough to make me stop doing projects.

And I did stop. I decided he was right, that things could wait. Life is too short to be miserable and injured. I didn't want my children avoiding me because I was sweaty and cranky and covered in Sheetrock mud. I told myself I'd never start another project. I'd been burned, literally, one time too many.

But, before long, the projects were calling me again. I heard our dreary old garage begging for a bright coat of paint. The cracks in the Sheetrock screamed at me and it would be nice to add a couple of new storage shelves. A piece of cake, I thought. All I'd need to do is buy paint and a little Sheetrock mud then . . .

Oh my. I don't think I can resist. Please don't tell my husband!

The hole *before* the 31 bags of concrete

# CHAPTER SEVEN

# Spare Parts

There's always one nut left over.

# He's Not That Into Me

by
## Stacey Gustafson

Hiring a good handyman is as tough as trying to lick your elbow. Heck, finding my husband was faster, easier and less expensive. Unfortunately, my husband doesn't do home improvement projects in his spare time. A combination of long hours at work and heavy air travel convinced him to leave home repairs to the experts.

After moving into our new house, I Googled "Handyman Services" and found match ups like eHandyman.com and ChristianHandyGuy.com. I had to act fast. Our 20-year-old house was crumbling around us. We needed help before we had to sleep in a tent or move in with our parents.

*Send me an angel,* I secretly prayed to the home-improvement gods.

The first guy I called was your typical older, retired jack-of-all-trades, anxious to earn extra money.

"Hi, I'm Stacey," I gushed, opening the front door. "You

won't believe how glad I am to see you." *Hallelujah!*

"What's the problem?" he said, all business.

We discussed the most critical project on the list—the replacement of broken and missing bathroom tiles. After the discussion, I hired him. The job lasted more than two weeks. He showed up daily, grinding and drilling to completion.

"Thank so much. You're the best," I said, laying on compliments as thick as pea soup.

A good man is hard to find.

By week three, he offered a helping hand with a series of minor projects. He hung pictures, fixed a leaky sink and cleaned out the garage. I called him at home the next week to help set up Christmas decorations and lights—the works.

But his attitude changed by week six. I had a sneaky feeling he was cheating on me. He turned up late for our next appointment. And he started taking calls on his cellphone during work.

"Yeah sure, I'll be over in 15," he said, whispering into the phone now cupped in his hand.

*What's this? Where's he think he's going? Who's he talking to?* I brooded.

With nary an explanation, he hiked up his tool belt, grabbed his tool box and skedaddled. I waited a few days before I called him again.

"This is Joe. Leave a message," said his voicemail.

"Joe, please call me. I need you for several small projects. I could really use your help. Thanks."

Weeks passed. Finally he dropped by to collect his last check. "By the way, I'm raising my rates and I'll be tied up a few months with a big job."

Did my handyman just dump me?

After Joe, I found Rusty through his online website, RustyDoesJobs.com. Based on his profile pic, he didn't look like a mass murderer. Best yet, he could start the next day.

He arrived 15 minutes early. I answered the door wearing ratty sweatpants and my old high school sweatshirt.

"Hi, I'm Rusty. You needed a handyman?" he said, looking me up and down.

*Hey, Buddy. Take a picture, it lasts longer!* I thought, not happy he arrived early for our date.

Once he put his eyes back in his head, he began the first job, hanging a ceiling fan in the den. From the top of the ladder, he asked, "How far do you want the fan to hang down?"

"I don't care," I said, tugging on my ear.

"Six inches or 12 inches?" he asked, with narrow, squinty eyes.

"Uh, I don't care." *Stop pressuring me.*

He settled on 12 inches. Then I proceeded to talk. I couldn't be stopped. I had no idea if he even answered me. "Did you watch the Giant's game?" "Can you believe the weather?" "How long have you been a handyman?" "My last handy guy never called me back. I think he's avoiding me."

"No kidding," he said, letting out a gasp.

When he finished replacing the fan then repairing the toilet, he said to use PayPal to pay him, grabbed his things and rushed out.

"Wait. Can I just mail you a check?"

"I don't use snail mail."

*He's afraid to give me his address.* "I guess this is goodbye?!"

I yelled after him, receiving no answer in return. *Another one bites the dust.*

Then my lucky day arrived. My realtor introduced me to Jose and the heavens split open. He had all the necessary qualities—loyalty, hardworking, strength and sensitivity. A match made in honey-do heaven.

Whatever the task, Jose proved to be an expert. And he listened and respected my opinion. "Tell me what you need," he said, leaning forward and giving me steady eye contact.

"I don't know how to store all this junk in the garage," I said.

"No worries. I'll build you shelves."

When his cellphone rang he said, "Lo siento. I'm with a customer. Call you later."

At the end of the day, he asked, "If you have a problem, I can come back Sunday."

"Wow, I really appreciate that." I smiled. "I'll be OK."

"Make your list then. See you Tuesday."

*Yeah! He likes me! He really likes me.* This was the beginning of a beautiful DIY relationship.

Stacey and Jose

# Awl in the Family

by
## Mike McHugh

Most times, when I talk to other men, they eventually get around to telling me about the latest project they're working on around the house. I don't know what it is that makes men want to do their own home improvements rather than hire a contractor. We're not this way about other professional services. I mean, when's the last time you've heard somebody brag about his do-it-yourself dentistry?

I think it's something in our genes. Not all men are this way, mind you, but most are. It appears to run in families. There's a problem, though, in that for any given family, there seems to be only a limited amount of do-it-yourself DNA to go around. And it's not evenly distributed. At least, it isn't in my family.

In our case, the bulk of the handyman genes went to my two younger brothers, Steve and Dan. They're so handy that they've been known to break things on purpose just to show off how good they are at fixing them. If they were shipwrecked on a desert island together, they could, using only palm fronds and bamboo stalks, construct a residence that would befit the Prince of Wales. It would even have a bowling alley.

Even though I'm the oldest, I got only a splash from that particular gene pool. It was just enough to make me want to work on my house, particularly since I'm too cheap to hire a contractor. On the other hand, it was too little to keep me from turning even the simplest chore into a train wreck.

A case in point is the doghouse I once built. My dog took one look at it and got himself an apartment.

So where does that leave me? Well, for the longest time, it left me begging my brothers to come over and do my projects for me. It did not shame me to do this. After all, it isn't my fault that they got all the talent. And besides, I bribe them with beer.

Now don't get me wrong. It wasn't like I'd just sit back and watch the *Beavis and Butthead* marathon on MTV while they did all the work. No, these were the days before *Beavis and Butthead*. But it's not just that. I did pitch in and help however I could. Granted, my capabilities were limited, but I could do some things. For instance, I'm really good at demolition—I could do it in my sleep. Come to think of it, I have. Once, when I was sleeping on the sofa, I rolled onto the floor and knocked over a half-empty beer bottle. The beer got into a floor outlet and fried the TV that was plugged into it.

I used my demolition skills a lot when I was in my first

house. It was a "handyman special," so called because the previous owner fancied himself as being quite handy. Unfortunately, he wasn't blessed by heredity, either, and so my brothers and I had our hands full tearing out all of his do-it-yourself projects. There were projects installed on top of projects, I kid you not. While remodeling the dining room, we tore out the crown molding, only to reveal more crown molding underneath, which itself had been laid over additional crown molding. We could have added on a garage using just the crown molding.

Another thing that I could handle was going to the hardware store. The way most do-it-yourself projects go, I'm surprised that Home Depot doesn't run a shuttle service. I myself could keep a driver busy all day long, given my propensity for getting the wrong thing then having to go back and return it. When we were working on the dining room, my brothers sent me to buy some compound to seal the joints in the new drywall. I returned with maybe enough to fill the tack holes from the pictures we'd taken down. And that pretty much ruined the rest of that workday, as Steve and Dan found it difficult to pick themselves up off the floor after that little mistake.

Some years later, I was transferred out of town and had to sell the house. This left me without my home improvement lifeline, but I was OK with that. By then, I felt like I'd done enough work with Steve and Dan to have picked up on some of the basics. I just needed to understand my limitations. Carpentry was fine, just no plumbing or electrical work. My mantra became, "If nothing flows through it, I can do it."

Still, I decided that I was through with handyman specials. And so I stressed to my realtor that I wanted my new house to be "in move-in condition." This is a term that means different things to different people. To my realtor, it meant that the condition of the roof should not be an issue, so long as I moved in on a sunny day.

Leaky roofs can be managed with a few strategically placed buckets, but not front doors. I can't remember why the one in my new house needed to be replaced. Maybe my wife decided she didn't like the one that came with the house, since it clashed with the welcome mat. It was one of those designer welcome mats that came from the Beyond section of Bed Bath & Beyond. So it was the door that had to go.

I assessed the project and since it would not involve unscrewing the doorbell, I concluded it was within my skill set. And so, early one Saturday morning, I set out to fetch my tool box and get to work. By lunchtime, I found the tool box, and so I commenced removing the offensive door.

There's one thing about replacing an exterior door that, in retrospect, is quite obvious, but which had escaped me at the time. Once you get to where the old door is off, you are committed for the duration. And the clock is running. You've got to have that new door on by dark or even earlier if you live in a neighborhood that has a lot of people peddling magazine subscriptions.

Given my knack for turning simple tasks into federal projects, things got kind of dicey as the day wore on. By late afternoon, I still wasn't anywhere close to having the new door hung. I was flying by the seat of my pants, and I knew it. I was going to crash and burn if I didn't think of something quick. And then it came to me—I'll just call my brother, Dan. Surely, he could talk me through to a smooth landing.

His voice was calm. "We're going to take this one step at a time," he said. "Together, we'll get you through this. Now, I need to ask you, do you have any shims?"

"Look, Dan," I answered, "I'm trying to hang a door here, not make my confession. And besides, you're no choir boy yourself."

"No, no," Dan replied. "I said 'shims,' not 'sins.' You're going to need to shim the door so that it's square in the frame." I was now picking up a hint of sarcasm in his tone. I was hoping he hadn't tied Steve in on the line to listen in.

In a scene reminiscent of the movie *Airplane*, we had some bumps and bruises. Yet, with Dan's help, we came to a happy ending. I got the new door hung, just as I noticed in the corner of my eye a college-aged lad approaching from down the block with an armful of magazines.

That night, I thought about my third brother, John. He did not get a single molecule of the family allotment of do-it-yourself DNA. In many ways, he's the lucky one. He shows about as much interest in home repairs as a potted plant does in the writings of Goethe. His highest achievement was to operate a can of spray paint when the number on his house had faded. Other than that, he just lets nature take its course. I haven't been to his house lately, but I bet he has more than a few strategically placed buckets.

As for me, I'm cursed for life. I've got all of the desire, but none of the talent. In retrospect, I'm like an altar boy at a Texas barbecue on Good Friday.

Mike and the door

# Monument
# to Manhood

by
### Cindy Hval

Our four sons are industrious diggers. When I tumbled into a crater they'd dug in our backyard, using plastic sand shovels and a broken rake, my husband, Derek, decided drastic measures were in order. Once they've had a taste of digging, boys—like dogs—are difficult to train.

Derek eyed the holey ground speculatively, "This area is just wasted space. I'd hate for you to fall in another hole. Honey, what we need here is a shed."

"We have a shed," I said, pointing to the rusty metal thing next to the house.

"Too small," Derek replied.

My husband is a man without a garage. A man without a garage is a sad thing. A woman married to a man without a garage is even sadder, for she must trip over fishing poles and climb over cross-country skis to reach her good china.

"I could build a shed," he announced, explaining he

could build it in the evenings when he got home from work. Derek continued, "Just think of all the space you'd have downstairs if my tools and fishing gear were in a shed." After 21 years of marriage, Derek was wise in the husbandly ways of getting what he wanted—he did this by pointing out the advantages for me.

When the shed plans arrived by FedEx, I realized Derek's idea of a shed was much different than mine. When he said, "build," I heard, "put together a prefab from Sears in one easy weekend." I need to get my hearing checked.

Excitedly, Derek poured over the architectural drawings and eagerly watched the accompanying DVD, *How to Build a Better Barn*. That's when I started to get nervous. "Barn? What happened to shed? How much is this going to cost?" I asked.

Big mistake. My husband can spout figures like an accountant on caffeine overload. By the time he was done with his number crunching and explaining, I was convinced we'd be losing money if we didn't build it.

Phone calls were made to his father and brother-in-law and the two "consultants" arrived. Since they are both native Norwegians, the consultation involved many cups of coffee, much pacing around the backyard and innumerable murmurs of, "Ya, ya." They dumped loads of crushed rock to level the area and hauled in stacks of lumber from Home Depot. This was no ordinary shed— according to the plans, this would be a "Colonial Cedar Textured Shed with Natural Cedar Trim." All I knew was that our unfinished second bathroom would remain unfinished, our dining room wouldn't get painted and I would have a lot of time to myself each evening.

The construction began. Neighbors leaned over the fence and wandered into the backyard, in the grip of shed envy. A photographer stopped by to snap a new mug shot for my newspaper column, but his eyes kept straying out the back window. "I'm sorry," he said, "But is that a barn in your backyard?"

"No," I sighed, "My husband is building a shed."

He stood transfixed and gazed at Derek's masterpiece. "Now, that's a shed!" His eyes clouded. "I wish I had a shed like that."

I finally got his attention long enough to take my photo, but I could tell he'd rather have been shooting the shed.

Weeks passed and this Monument to Manhood now stands a few shingles and a door away from being complete. Curious that he was almost done with the project, I asked Derek when he was going to buy the door.

"Buy?" Derek gasped, "I'm not going to buy the door. I'm going to make it."

*Of course he is*, I said to myself as I walked away.

Eight months into the project, I'm still tripping over fishing poles and skis, but I haven't fallen into any holes. The boys have been too busy to dig. Dad has had them painting the shed and hauling shingles.

A thought crossed my mind the other day: *Maybe we should wire this shed shrine for electricity. I could then make it the new "time-out" destination.* I smiled to myself over the idea. Whenever I need a break from all the testosterone in our home, I could banish one or all of the men in my family to the shed.

That nearly-done, barn-red building out back has definite appeal. Now that I think about it, every woman needs a shed.

Derek on top of the shed, with the boys not far behind.

# In Hot Water

by
## Gloria Hander Lyons

"What's that noise?" asked my husband, Bob, standing in the hallway outside our bedroom door. I walked over to stand beside him and cocked my head to one side for maximum audio reception.

It was definitely an unusual sound, like thousands of tiny metal beads trickling down inside the wall. I glanced up at the ceiling and experienced one of those light-bulb moments.

"The hot water heater!" I screeched. It was directly overhead in the attic. Those weren't beads tumbling down inside the wall—it was a waterfall!

We took the stairs two at a time and opened the attic door. Sure enough, there was a geyser shooting out the top of the hot water heater. It looked like Old Faithful.

"Turn it off!" I yelled.

"I can't," said Bob, dodging the spray, "there's no shut-off valve!"

He bounded down the stairs and out to the main line at the curb. I stood in the first-floor hallway and watched in horror as water seeped out underneath the baseboards, bubbled up through the carpet and pooled around my feet.

Bob yanked off the cover of the underground box and looked down into a black hole. Back he came in search of a flashlight, and then sprinted out to the curb once more. I was impressed. For 64, he was moving pretty darn fast.

Now he could see into the dark crevasse. It was as plain as day that the shut-off valve was covered under several inches of mud, which had dried to the consistency of concrete.

Bob dashed into the garage for a spade to chisel the dirt away from the handle. A jackhammer might have been a better choice, but he hadn't yet added that item to his stash of tools. Finally, he unearthed the critical knob, but it just wouldn't budge. By now, the water cascading down the walls was trickling out the backdoor.

Bob jumped up for another run on the tool cache in the house and bumped into me standing right behind him.

"I thought you might need this," I said, holding up a wrench. All do-it-yourself homeowners are well aware of the fact that you can fix anything with a wrench and duct tape.

I followed Bob back to the turn-off valve. Using the wrench, he twisted the valve closed and we both collapsed onto the grass.

Relieved that part of the ordeal was over, we looked at each other and broke out in giggles, thinking about our Keystone Kops routine. It must have been the adrenaline from all the excitement, but we felt victorious—another crisis averted through quick thinking, teamwork and skill.

The soggy carpet and waterlogged ceiling waiting for us inside, however, were another matter. But, unlike Scarlett O'Hara, we didn't have the luxury of thinking about that tomorrow. We placed an emergency call to a local plumbing company for a new hot water heater then spent the rest of the day hauling wet carpet and padding out to the driveway.

"Maybe we should install a ceramic-tile floor instead of carpet," I suggested, placing an 8-foot ladder below the drooping ceiling. I climbed up and used an ice pick to poke a hole in the Sheetrock to drain the remaining 5 gallons of water from the attic.

Bob slid a bucket underneath to catch the stream. "That's a great idea. I've always wanted one of those tile-cutting saws. Let's head over to Home Depot as soon as the plumbers are finished."

And just like that, we were off and running again on a brand-new DIY adventure.

Home sweet home—definitely not for the faint of heart!

# Project Man

by
Maggie Lamond Simone

"Well, hon, looks like we need to find a roofer!" my husband announced, phone book in hand. I couldn't help feeling he was just a little too perky about it. In my mind, it was just wrong to spend that much money on something I can neither wear nor drive. But he's a project man, and a project man is simply not happy unless there is major construction happening in or around his home on a regular basis.

It started last winter when the combination of record snowfall and subzero temperatures in our town created an interesting dilemma. Should we shovel the roof or simply incorporate the rivulets of water streaming down our living room walls into the general decorating scheme?

After some debate, we pulled out the phone book and found a young man to shovel off the roof—and that's exactly what he did. He shoveled off our roof, shingles and all. Unfortunately, most of the shingles, in their dramatic escape from Shovel Boy, chose to sail into our landscaping. As I gazed at the stump and branch that were once my beautiful hemlock, I nearly wept. Such a young life, cut short by a convoy of fleeing shingles. It wasn't fair.

"And as long as we're replacing the roof, let's redo the landscaping, too," my husband said, opening the dreaded, but to him, magical *Yellow Pages*. "We'll put in a little patio over by the deck. It'll have paver bricks and a walkway and little lights and you'll love it!" His idea was a miracle, really—a little hemlock growing into a big patio.

But was my husband content now? Not so much. As our new roof was being installed and our yard undergoing reconstructive surgery, my husband said, "That sure is a nice-looking roof and yard. Let's paint the house!" And off he went to find the phone book. I really have stopped trying to understand him. It's just easier.

This newest project sparked the great family debate as to the perfect color for the house. My husband and I favored a neutral, non-glow-in-the-dark shade. Our daughter was happy with nothing less than Barbie pink, while our son chose camouflage, proving once again that my goals and desires for my children are essentially meaningless in the face of biology.

"Hey, Mag, did you ever notice we don't have a storm door?" my husband asked excitedly the following week. Fortunately, the new door we apparently had to buy to go with the new paint job was easy enough to match, because hey, what doesn't go with camouflage?

"Now about the playroom," came out of his mouth next. This suggestion actually perked me up.

The playroom, you see, was my pride and joy. It was a wonderful, large open space painted in primary colors that provided our children a safe place to play and me, a room with a door in which to shove all their toys.

Unfortunately, it also had a drop ceiling, which, well, dropped. *Kaboom!* One day it was a ceiling, the next it was a floor. Playdates became a little tricky: "Yes, your child will be playing in there, but I'm sure those hanging wires and things aren't really dangerous"

We decided that if we ever expected our kids to have friends, a ceiling was crucial. Once the new ceiling was in, naturally, the room had to be repainted. This was unexpected since I had just painted it last year. "No problem!" said my husband. "Really! It'll be fun! We'll just get the kids their own little brushes, and they can help!" Uh-huh. What's that saying about some path and good intentions?

At any rate, I think we're getting there, although there may be a few wrap-up projects yet to do. I came home the other day and "The Book" was open to "Driveways," because you really can't have a new roof without a new driveway. And, of course, we have to replace those pesky outside lights, which no longer coordinated with the house because of the new paint job. With the fixtures up, we were finally done.

Then just today, my husband walked in with some new home listings and said, "I don't know, I guess I'm just getting a little bored. Wouldn't it be fun to just look around a bit, see what's out there?"

I simply smiled, picked up the phone book and hurled it at him. He ducked, looked back at the new hole in the wall, and said happily, "You know what? You're right. There's still plenty to do around here!"

# In Pursuit of Perfection

by
Timothy Martin

When it comes to long, grueling events, forget seven-day races and runs across the continent. For a real test of endurance, try remodeling a bedroom closet with your father-in-law.

That was the task my wife laid out for me when her parents came to visit. To be honest, I wasn't up to the job. It involved tearing out walls, rewiring outlets, moving pipes, spackling, painting and even moving a water heater. It also involved using precious time that I could spend watching my favorite baseball team—the San Francisco Giants—play the Oakland A's.

It's not that I don't like my father-in-law. He's a great guy. He's also a darn good carpenter. Put a saw and a piece of wood in Frank's hands and cuts are ruler straight. When he joins two pieces of wood, they always fit perfectly. Frank believes in doing a job right. That's the part that troubled me. I have little patience for home improvement. When I hang a door, it hangs crooked. My cabinets resemble Picasso paintings and my faucets spout water higher than Old Faithful. I don't care about craftsmanship. I just want to get the job done.

Realizing my shoddy work habits wouldn't set well with her dad, my wife asked me to mend my ways, at least temporarily. For the next week I was to forget about ballgames and do exactly what my father-in-law asked. In short, I was to be the perfect helper.

There's nothing like a little home renovation to take your mind off baseball. My tactic on the first day was to watch the Giants play before Frank showed up. But my father-in-law arrived early, rushed back to the bedroom and immediately began taking measurements for the closet. He wanted to get right to work.

I watched Frank closely. I fetched wood, nails and whatever else he needed. As he worked, I couldn't help but notice how long it took him to accomplish each task. Fifteen minutes to measure a board. Ten minutes to cut it. A full 30 minutes to decide where to install the plumbing. My emotions swelled and crashed like teenage mood swings. I wanted the job to go faster, but Frank's attention to detail was absolute. It was bone-deep and forever-lasting. I wanted to see how my team was doing, but I knew better. I realized then it was as good a day as any to wean myself from America's favorite pastime.

On the afternoon of the second day, my father-in-law asked me to cut a piece of wood. Black fear seized my vitals. I wasn't a carpenter, but I did as instructed. Throwing caution to the wind, I snatched up the saw and started cutting. When Frank held the board in place, he shook his head. It was off by an inch.

"You have to do it again," he said.

"Why?" I asked.

"Because it doesn't fit right."

"So?" I said.

Frank stared at me. "You don't want the closet to turn out lopsided, do you?"

*It doesn't matter*, I thought, biting my tongue. *I just want the job to be done.*

Four boards later, a miracle of sorts. My cut was straight. The board fit perfectly. But the job had taken its toll. My brain felt worn down to the knuckles. Worse yet, I had gone two full days without watching a single ballgame. The job moved slower than geological plate-shifting.

One night, I dropped into bed completely spent. I dreamed that Frank and I were working on the closet and the World Series was about to begin. It was the Giants verses the Dodgers. I really wanted to watch the game. Frank kept measuring a board that needed to be cut. He measured again. And again. And again. It was board-measuring Groundhog Day. I kept saying, "It's good, Frank. It's fine." But he wouldn't listen. He just kept measuring and re-measuring the board. I woke up screaming and in a cold sweat.

The next day, I complained to my wife. "Your dad is taking way too long," I told her. "We should have finished the closet long ago."

"He's trying to do a good job," she replied. "If you were half the carpenter he is, maybe you'd understand." *Owww! Kick a guy when he's down, why don't you!*

Time went into one of its long, slow, taffy-like stretches.

The days blurred and I had to concentrate to keep them in sequence. Then an odd thing happened. At some point between the spackling and trim, I measured a board once, twice, three times. Without realizing what I was doing, I made sure the board was the proper length. A strange combination of understanding and shame dawned on me, coming on like a rheostat-controlled light in a darkened theater. The closet was almost done and it looked great. I was actually proud. Frank and I were just putting on the finishing touches when I noticed the doors still needed knobs. "I'll put on those knobs," I told Frank.

"Why don't you watch the ballgame," he said. "I'll finish up."

The words clotted on my tongue like lint spun out of a dryer, but I actually replied, "That's OK, Frank. The game can wait."

# CHAPTER EIGHT

# Better Lawns and Gardens

Send in the gnomes.

# Rock of Ages

by
## John Schlimm

After my best friend Steven's great grandmother passed away, he bought her little farmhouse out in the country. She had built the house 50 years earlier, and like many in her generation, she didn't throw anything away. Eventually, the inside became overcrowded with a lifetime of trinkets and books and furniture. Likewise, the outside shrubs and lawn grew wildly and freely.

When it came time to transform the house into a new home, Steven enlisted my help, as well as that of other family members and friends. With elbow grease and several Mr. Clean Magic Erasers, the inside was a snap to clean. But the outside is where the true do-it-yourself treasure was awaiting, just beneath our feet.

While we were sitting on the front porch one morning, Steven said to me, "You know, I think there are bricks under the front yard. Before this porch was here, my great grandma used this area as her driveway. She'd pull her car right up to the front door."

*Here it comes*, I thought. With Steven, there is never a dull moment—or a still moment. He always has to be in motion.

It was about 8 A.M.

Steven hopped up from his chair, grabbed a small handheld shovel and bounded down the steps. He hunched over and gently proceeded to lift the grass in front of the steps, as if peeling back a carpet. Sure enough, he discovered a layer of colorful gold-and-red bricks underneath.

"Let's make a walkway from the driveway to the steps," Steven suggested, with an enthusiastic smile. I had never done anything like that, but I'm always game for a new adventure.

Soon, the two of us, along with Steven's mom, were carefully wedging shovels and picks under the grass, unfastening the roots that had taken hold of the bricks. We rolled back large clumps of grass, exposing the aged treasure underneath. The sod would be saved and used later to line the driveway. Nothing would be wasted.

By 1 P.M., a welcoming "new" sidewalk that was decades old invited visitors to stroll up onto the wooden front porch. It was beautiful, and I was now looking forward to relaxing. I never knew lifting up grass could be so intense!

"You know," Steven said, "the rest of the front yard is also full of bricks under the grass."

I braced myself. Just when I thought the workday was over, I could suddenly hear the *Jaws'* theme music playing in my head. The work shovel was once more coming for me. *Dunt, dunt . . . dunt, dunt, dunt, dunt . . .*

"And your point?" I hazarded.

"Let's build a patio out back!" Steven exclaimed. A small 5-foot by 7-foot cement slab off the backdoor was all that existed.

"Why not," I replied. After all, being the workout junkie I am, I thought about the great additional workout I'd get from hauling all the wheelbarrow loads of bricks around to the back of the house. Add to that the exercise from painstakingly unearthing them all with small shovels and picks. And I knew Steven's job would be to actually place the bricks on the ground and design the patio. He's very particular about such things, so we figured we'd just leave that job up to him.

"First, we need a layer of sand, so the patio will be even," Steven instructed.

"How do you know about these things?" I asked in amazement. "I would have just started throwing the bricks down."

"I don't know how I know, I just do. Now will you please bring about 30 wheelbarrow loads of sand over here? There's a sand pile back by the barn," he said, again with a smile.

*Yes, sir!* I thought. I practically saluted this general of backyard DIY-ers. Instead, I rolled my eyes and smiled back.

An extra workout, indeed! Steven's mom and I delivered the sand in about two hours' time, and then headed to the front.

It was now 3:30 P.M.

Over the course of the next six or so hours, we hauled about 50 wheelbarrow loads of bricks around back where Steven's patio was taking shape. Each time, we were careful to replace the temporarily uprooted grass so that it looked untouched. Unless told, no one would know of the cache the front lawn had surrendered.

"Will you please put the bricks in piles according to shape and size?" Steven-the-General requested.

By now, my arms felt as though they might fall off. *What we wouldn't do for our friends*, I thought, laughing to myself. Even my smiling muscles were sore by this point! However, we obliged. Whole bricks went on one pile, long bricks on another and broken chunks on yet another pile. This made it easier for Steven to pick and choose the appropriate bricks as needed. And it taught me that DIY really is all about organization and sweat and sore muscles.

I marveled at my best friend, the amateur bricklayer. Each of the hundreds of bricks was examined then carefully placed. It was like he was assembling a giant puzzle. Every brick fit perfectly where he put it, as if it had been custom-made for that particular spot on earth.

By 10 P.M., beneath the back porch light, a stunning, curved mosaic of brick spread out from the cement slab.

"It's amazing!" I exclaimed. "Who would have thought this was possible—and in a day!" Famished, we moved a table and chairs onto the center of the patio, the grill onto a side wing of the patio Steven had created just for it, and an antique chiminea—a rounded pot sometimes used as a stove—from his great grandmother's barn added an authentic country accent in the corner. By 11 P.M., we were enjoying a cookout on the new patio, under the stars and by the warmth of a fire.

Along with the front sidewalk, the patio was an addition that may have cost thousands of dollars if outsourced, but had, instead, been bought and paid for with good old-fashioned sweat, time, ingenuity and friendship. Not to mention a treasure that had been buried like a time capsule, just waiting for its time in the sun once more.

Steven and his brick patio

# Thou Shalt Not

by
Shari Courter

Several years ago, my husband bought me a weed-whacker for Mother's Day. I'll let that sink in for a moment. My Mother's Day gift was a weed-whacker.

It's not that I'm complaining about being the one who did all the yardwork. And I'm not the type that always expects a gift, but something about opening that weed-whacker on Mother's Day didn't sit well with me. It didn't help when my husband saw the look on my face and said, "This one doesn't plug in, so it will make your life a lot easier."

*No, what would make my life a lot easier is if YOU did the yardwork,* I thought. But I didn't say that out loud.

The biggest problem with the make-my-life-a-lot-easier weed-whacker was that I couldn't start it. Clearly, this super-easy weed-whacker was made for a man, but little did they know. Since it doesn't plug in, it contains a tank for gas that rests under the handle and adds about 5 extra pounds to the machine. Since I could no longer simply turn it on by using a switch—like I had with my old one—I had to figure out a way to balance the contraption on one leg, hold the handle steady and trigger down with my right hand, and yank a pull cord as hard as I could with my left hand. *Gee, that does make my life easier!* I sarcastically said to myself while struggling to start the machine.

The bottom line is that I could not start that freakin' weed-whacker by myself. I had to beckon my husband outside every time I needed to start it, a process that entailed waiting for him to put something on—other than his boxer shorts—and trudge outside, while loudly commenting, "It's really hot out here." To make matters worse, I also lacked the capacity to keep the stupid thing running after he started it. It wouldn't die right away, mind you. It waited until he was back on the couch in his boxers.

Every.

Single.

Time.

That was 2008. The next Mother's Day—in 2009—I did the yardwork after church. No complaints. I find it relaxing to ride the lawnmower around an acre of land, wearing my bathing suit in the warm sun. I don't even mind push mowing the trim, as I chalk that up to productive cardio. But then it came time to drag out that horrible piece of machinery. My nemesis. That freakin' weed-whacker. Notice the term "weed-whacker" never stands alone anymore.

I made the same mistake I always made. I attempted to start it by myself, repeatedly. Until I was hot, sweaty and pissed. I screamed my husband's name in my most terrifying demon voice and waited for him to appear. Round two of our ritual began. He started that freakin' weed-whacker and just as he disappeared into the house, it died.

That's when I completely lost it. The meltdown to end all meltdowns took place right there in the front yard, in my bathing suit, on Mother's Day. I had a knock-down, drag-out, F-bomb dropping, testimony-losing tantrum and I literally beat the shit out of that freakin' weed-whacker.

A couple minutes later, standing there panting and dripping with sweat, was when I heard it—the *clippety cloppety* sounds of horses' hooves on the road directly behind me. I slowly turned around to see a caravan of Amish families trekking by our house with hands over their children's ears, their mouths agape with horrified looks on their faces, thus forever confirming their stance against technology. *Glad I could help!*

I don't do the yardwork anymore. Not just because of that incident, although that certainly contributed. Somehow after that, I lost my yardwork mojo. I started running into things with the riding mower and my husband had to change the mower's blades four times. And I lost focus. I stopped noticing our son's golf balls scattered in the grass and needless to say, things got dangerous out there.

My husband finally put his foot down and announced that he would be doing the yardwork from then on. So far, he's lived up to that promise, with exception of one thing. He has yet to use that freakin' weed-whacker.

Shari, the freakin' weed-whacker and some Amish friends . . .

# A Zillion Zinnias

by
Terri Elders

I still remember how Ken's voice spiked with exhilaration when I picked up the phone in my Washington, D.C. cubicle that gray spring morning all those years ago.

"I finally found our dream house, baby. It's out in the country, with over three acres of land. There are evergreens, apple trees, a stable and two fenced pastures. We'll plant tons of flowers. I want color everywhere."

"Make an offer," I urged. We'd been scouting around Stevens County in northeast Washington for over a year.

When Ken called back, he still sounded elated. "Go ahead and give notice. We'll move the end of June. Hey, the slogan up here is 'near nature, near perfect.' You've got to believe it!"

Since we'd been married, we'd lived in a town house with a garden patch not much bigger than a terrarium. With all this new space, we could grow crocus and narcissus to jumpstart the spring, Asian lilies and gladiola to brighten the summer and marigolds and zinnias to carry us through the waning months of autumn. I pictured our retirement home filled with vases of cut flowers. I'd plant pansies, petunias, peonies. Back to nature! Back to the land! The dormant hippie in me shivered with bliss.

A few months later when we pulled into the circular driveway of our new home, Ken must have seen my face fall. Though the house itself lived up to his description, the yard was overgrown with weeds and woody bushes. The only color I spotted came from dandelions nearly the size of sunflowers. In front, several poplar trees seemed to suffer from some fatal arboreal disease, and the listless lilacs drooped.

"When Scott and Rick arrive next week we'll get rid of the dead trees and branches. You'll see. We'll have it landscaped in no time." My husband patted my hand.

I brightened. Ken's son, Scott, was a Master Gardener, and Rick made even the desert bloom in his Nevada backyard. The trio would saw, chop and prune, and my spirits would lift. Near nature, near perfect just might be attainable.

That fall I lugged home sacks of bulbs from a local nursery. That's when I discovered that even though we had plenty of space for flower beds, I couldn't dent the stony ground with spade, shovel or trowel.

"It's hopeless," I announced, tossing my sacks on the kitchen counter.

"Don't worry," Ken said. "We'll haul in topsoil."

The contractor who'd Sheetrocked our living room said his father would sell us some rich, fertile soil for a decent price. A few days later, the pair pulled up in a dump truck and started to unload.

Ken spent hours with his sketchpad, designing the flower beds. He poured through nursery catalogs and ordered plants guaranteed to grow in our chilly Zone 9. As they arrived, he planted the hydrangeas, astilbes, phlox and Asian lilies. Then I buried my bulbs—the crocus, gladiola and tulips—just ahead of the first frost.

All winter we gazed out at the snow, anticipating the spring thaw. We savored cocoa, exchanged stories of previous gardening adventures and chattered about the coming summer when we'd sip lemonade and admire bevies of butterflies and hummingbirds fluttering around our flower beds.

Ken spoke of the first house he bought when his sons were little, with soil so hard panned that the roots of trees couldn't break through. I recounted how I helped my mom plant the tropical bushes that I thought were "hot biscuits" until my big sister hissed that they were called "hibiscus." We laughed about the tiny, but lush, garden Ken had created behind our former town house and how it had flourished until our Akita puppy destroyed every green thing in it, turning it into a lunar landscape.

Then Ken admitted he hadn't realized the white-spored "wishies" in our pastures were dandelions gone to seed. And I confessed that the only flowers I'd ever coaxed from seed were backyard zinnias, and that was just before my son was born. That same year, barely out of my teens, I'd been so proud of producing both a baby and a garden.

We exchanged apprehensive glances. Maybe we weren't good candidates to become Master Gardeners, but our new garden surely would flourish, just like our millennial-year marriage.

By early April, shoots began to poke above the soil. We sauntered about, examining every green pinpoint.

"How do you tell the weeds from the valuable plants?" I asked.

Ken grinned. "Easy! If you tug and it emerges readily, it's

a valuable plant."

He sneaked a sideways peek at my frown, and then gave a more convincing answer. "Really, you just wait until you can see some kind of a leaf pattern. Besides, this is supposed to be great topsoil. Don't worry about weeds."

Then the green shoots morphed into wall-to-wall weeds. I spent one entire May weekend weeding, but by the following Saturday, every uninvited houseguest weed had returned, towing along several relatives.

And where were those plants Ken ordered from Florida, the ones guaranteed to grow in colder climes? A few Asian lilies shot up, along with a phlox or two and a single burning bush. That was it. Hundreds of dollars, and we had no hollyhocks, no keys of heaven, no variegated weigela. They hadn't survived the sub-zero temperatures of December.

The "near nature" part of that motto took on a different meaning, well past the fauna and flora definitions. We had fawns aplenty. I banished my childhood crush on Bambi, as hordes of deer descended from the surrounding hills to devour our gladiolas down to the ground. They even snapped off the blooms on every surviving lily.

We finally vanquished the weeds, but our garden plots remained bare. In a last-ditch effort, I sowed zinnia seeds. By late August, our garden glimmered with lavender, yellow, magenta, pink and fuchsia zinnias. The garden buzzed with the whirr of honeybees. I then added some daisy and iris plants to the mix. By Indian summer, the blooms from the towering zinnias filled every large vase we owned. A passerby even stopped her car to take a snapshot to send to her mother who, she claimed, was zany for zinnias.

Ken, though, started to favor flowering shrubs and over

the next few summers, coaxed me into surrendering space to them. He'd grown impatient with annuals, and especially with the time it took my zinnias to mature and bloom.

"You and those blasted zinnias," he'd growl, as I stubbornly defended my one remaining strip of garden.

"Remember that next September," I'd retort, "when they're the only flowers left."

I recently learned that zinnias sometimes are called "youth-and-old-age." I think of them as the Alpha and Omega, the first and the last, the flowers of my youth and now my old age, my dependable, reliable, Indian summer beauties. Their radiance warms my heart.

A widow now, I still live in our dream house . . . near nature, near perfect. I get through the icy winters by anticipating the months ahead and how the yards will burst into bloom with the riotous color of a zillion zinnias.

Terri's zinnias

# Muddy Waters

by
## Stephanie Fellenstein

A giant mud hole and a bad case of the hives taunted me for months, and it was all my husband's fault. Toward the end of winter, he came up with a grandiose plan for a new back patio. It included two levels made from reclaimed sidewalk pieces, with new benches and new shrubbery.

Two things made me agree to this craziness. One, he painted a beautiful picture with his words and I was intrigued. And two, the new patio would be the perfect setting for the garden-themed wedding shower I was throwing for my cousin in June.

"I think my friends and I can do most of the work ourselves," he said the day he hauled home a jackhammer.

That's when the rash started.

Our house is 80 years old. It was built, brick by brick, by a police-officer-turned farmer and his family. While the gentleman farmer may have been adept at many things, construction was not one of his strong suits. I'm pretty sure he eyeballed most of his measurements. Over the years, as the house settled, each wall shifted to a different angle, leaving numerous large cracks.

The cop-turned-farmer's bizarre craftsmanship is what prompted the patio makeover. For example, when he built the house, he poured a concrete sidewalk against one wall. After we move in, we soon learned that every winter the run-off from the gutters would drip onto the sidewalk. The water would freeze overnight and we would wake up to an icy, speed-skating lane from the backdoor to the garage, 50 feet away.

Excited by the patio makeover, my husband and the jack-hammer attacked the sidewalk with glee. He ripped off the back steps, pummeled the old porch and carted off the side-walk chunks. All that was left was a giant dirt hole. At this point in the project, his friends realized they were in way over their heads and left my husband alone to deal with the ensuing disaster.

Then it started raining and my rash got worse. It rained for days then weeks. The hole filled with water and the whole backyard turned to mud. The weather forecasters called it the wettest spring since 1870. I called it a disaster. The kids called it a pool.

The wedding shower date crept closer and closer.

"It just needs to dry out a little before we can start," my husband said.

Every time I pulled into the driveway and stopped next to the giant muddy hole, my neck itched. I tried to avert my eyes.

Since the backdoor was now across the pond, we had to use the front door which opened into the living room. The new pale green carpet we put down in the living room seemed like a good idea at the time. But that was before the never-ending mud hole. And if we were using the front door, our "mud-is-my-favorite-thing-in-the-whole-world" yellow lab Gus had to use the front door, too.

Most days, I could corral Gus on the front porch and clean him off before letting him into the house. The kids, however, were not as thorough when they let him in. It went something like this: Kid #1 would stand in the doorway waving a towel like a bullfighter while Kid #2 opened the front door, summoning the beast. Gus raced through the door and under the towel. *Voila!* Automatic dog wash. Not really.

One afternoon, I was working in my office when Gus came in to greet me—his pink tongue accentuated by the dark brown mud framing his whole face. I ran out of the room and followed a trail of muddy paw prints down the hallway, through the living room and into the kitchen, where it seems he had stopped for a drink. Then the paw prints continued through the dining room as Gus checked all his familiar spots before curling up in a big, muddy blob for a quick nap. I considered exiling the kids and the dog to the front porch for the duration of the project, but didn't want to tangle with children's services or the SPCA. That would only make my rash much worse.

Two days of sun finally allowed my husband to pour the concrete. Then we waited through another week of rain. The muddy chunks were leveled and the patio took shape. I sat outside on the ground, whispering sweet nothings to the grass seed, coaxing the tiny blades to grow.

The day of the wedding shower dawned bright and beautiful, with not a drop of rain in the forecast. Fat bunches of blue hydrangeas sat in Mason jars on each table under white tents. Shower guests mingled on the sandstone patio, commenting on the lovely backyard. I chuckled to myself, picturing the guests sitting in the giant mud hole, had the shower been a few weeks earlier.

Two years later, the grass has filled in nicely. It is thick and lush around the sandstone patio. Cool breezes blow over the hammock that hangs nearby.

"Hey honey, I was thinking about updating the kitchen," my husband said recently.

I scratched my neck.

The Fellenstein's new patio

# He Who Kills Weeds

by

## Stacey Gustafson

"If you're interested in keeping this job, you cannot speak to my husband," I said to Francisco, the new lawn-service guy. "If he asks you any questions, you must say, 'No hablo inglés.' Deal?"

"No problem. But why?" Francisco asked, scrunching his eyebrows.

"Do you have a minute?" I asked, rubbing the back of my neck and pointing to a folding chair. "Take a seat."

It all began eight years ago in Colorado. We used Crack-O-Dawn Lawn Service, but my husband, Mike, believed they were not doing enough to kill unwanted dandelions, daisies, crabgrass and thistles.

Mike announced, "I'm going to Home Depot to buy some Ortho Weed-B-Gon." He grabbed the car keys off the kitchen counter and away he went.

"Wait. You have to take a kid with you," I said, picking oatmeal bits off my T-shirt with a fingernail. "They've been driving me crazy all morning."

On cue, our five-year-old daughter kicked over a stack of books and spilled apple juice on the tile floor.

"I want ice cream!" she demanded, hands on hips.

"No," I said, taking a deep breath. "We just finished breakfast."

"Chocolate ice cream with sprinkles!" she wailed, thrusting her head backward.

"No," I repeated for the tenth time.

*Calgon, take me away,* I said to myself, dreaming about a long, hot soak in the tub with a glass of wine. Yes, I knew it was still morning.

Despite the kitchen chaos, our three-year-old son played with Duplo building blocks in the living room, quiet as a lamb. At least somebody was relaxed! He had no reaction to the conversation either way, but sweetly played with his favorite toys.

Mike's head swiveled between the kids—The Screamer and our son—just like a barn owl. He was trying to decide which one to take to the store with him. In a flash, he snatched our son off the ground, stuck him on his shoulder and headed for the door. My husband was no dummy. Our daughter's temper tantrums were legendary. She could hit decibel levels higher than the emergency alert system.

Mike returned home with his purchases and plunked our son in his crib for a nap. Then, with weed killer clenched in his sweaty fist, he scooted outside and attacked the lawn with the vengeance of Attila the Hun. For hours, Mr. Thorough sprayed the deadly weeds, vigilant not to miss a spot. Finally finished and pleased with his work, Mike showered and plopped in front of the television for a little R&R.

But in a few days, our lush, bright green Zoysia grass transformed into a smoky gray-green color and large patches turned sandy brown and crunchy. During his usual service appointment, Joe, the owner of Crack-O-Dawn, rang our doorbell. "Lady, something's wrong with your grass," he said, shaking his head.

"Oh, don't worry," I reassured him with a toss of my ponytail. "My husband sprayed it good with Weed-B-Gon."

"It is killing more than weeds," he said through narrowed eyes. "Show me what he used."

I rummaged around in the garage until I found the spray bottle. Joe's eyes opened wide. "Did you read the label? This is bad. I've never seen it happen before." He paused. "Is he here?"

I hollered through the rear door for He-Who-Kills-Weeds to meet us in the garage.

The two of us stood with our heads down as Joe admonished us. "Sir, you used total vegetation killer, not weed killer. This stuff seeps into the area, 12 inches deep by 12 inches in circumference, killing everything in its way." Flipping a hand in dismissal, he said, "You'll have to dig it all out."

When Joe left, my better-half crumpled into the reclining chair and said, "Never say a word about this to anyone. Promise?"

"No problema."

*I won't tell anyone. I'll tell everyone.*

Later that day, he shoveled dirt out of the affected areas. After seven days of excavation, our yard looked like the scene in the movie *Holes* where the juvenile detainees shoveled pits in the desert to "build character."

News of our predicament spread in our cul-de-sac as fast

as gossip at an all-girls high school. Neighbors sauntered past our lot with their small children and pets. I could almost hear them say, "That's the house I told you about. It's a real shame what happened."

It took two years for our lawn to recover, but my husband pinky-swore never to fertilize, aerate, kill weeds or pick daisies again when we moved to our new home in California. "Look, no touch" was his new motto.

When I finished my story, Francisco shrugged his shoulders, "Oh, this is the reason I can't talk to your husband?"

"That's right."

But in his defense, Mike said he made the "big mistake" because of our young son, that he had distracted him that day at Home Depot, the day he bought the wrong product. I bet next time he goes shopping, he takes The Screamer.

Mike holding son Brock and standing with The Screamer (daughter Ashley)

# It Had to Be Yew

by
Lesley Morgan

My husband turned into a gardener last weekend, just to please me. Left to his own devices, picking up a trowel or a cultivating tool is one of the last things he'd choose to do. Ever. It ranks right up there with fly fishing and decoupage.

We recently moved to a slightly neglected home in a town close to my husband's new job. Most of the summer had passed when a sizeable patch of our front lawn turned the color of dun and blew away with the wind. We didn't have to search far for a cause. Our clue was the half-dozen bags of Grub Max covered by a tarp in the garage. Sadly, we had moved in too late in the season to nip the grubs in the bud . . . uh, larva stage. Our grubs, apparently, were in full party mode. They were dancing in the dirt and had blown up to the size of woolly caterpillars.

We decided to cure the grub situation with a three-pronged approach: dead grass removal, grub neutralizing chemicals and a combination of sod and reseeding. The area in question was roughly half the size and shape of a pitcher's mound, large enough to require some serious cash.

Somewhere on a joyride between our southern New Hampshire home and Boston, I'd come up with the great idea of saving money by removing a patch of grass on a sharp incline near our front steps. It was a particularly pesky area to mow, requiring substantial upper-body strength to maneuver our aged Lawn Boy around the retaining wall rocks that jutted up like a mini mountain range. We called it the "goat strip," even though the covenants in our subdivision outlawed our owning livestock. To use it as sod was a burst of Yankee ingenuity and thrift. In its place, I figured we would plant a bunch of shrubs purchased from our area's premier garden center, using the welcome-to-the-neighborhood $25 gift card they'd mailed us soon after our arrival.

Early Saturday morning, we measured and I sketched. After coming up with a plan for a modest landscape project, we headed off to Paradise Gardens. We were admiring some gracefully nodding evergreens and weeping fruit trees when Bill shot out of the office like a car salesman on Presidents' Day. He offered to help us with our selection of plant material and grew really enthusiastic when he saw the sketch of the soon-to-be de-sodded plot.

Together, we came up with a magic number of five. We needed five plants of various colors, textures and shapes. I liked the mop-headed cypress, which was the name of the lacy, chartreuse evergreen that overflowed a display bed. With a long face, Bill lamented, "Out of stock." He then pointed to a blue star juniper, a bird's nest spruce, a lanky, red-leafed bush called a "ninebark" and a curly, petite arborvitae that resembled a green coral formation. *Is it a yew?* I wondered to myself.

We collectively admired a half-acre of plants. At some point during the show and tell, we were so lulled into a dreamy green state of landscaping bliss that I couldn't help but exclaim, "Spirea, sumac and spruce—oh my!"

However, we weren't so far gone that we couldn't help but notice the price tags. Yikes! The juniper was the size of a cabbage and priced at $58.95, the same for the 16-inch holly. At this rate, we'd have to take out a second mortgage to finance a fully re-landscaped yard. So we settled on three shrubs instead of five and told Bill that we'd wait until the following spring to purchase the cypress and a golden euonymus, which was also out of stock.

Talk about sticker shock. After our discount, we still owed Paradise Gardens $140. It was more than double what we had planned to spend. By then, in good conscience, we couldn't back out. So we loaded our precious plants into the trunk and headed home to do the real work.

We measured our roughly triangular work site to be 9 foot by 28 foot or about 210 square feet, which sounded small. But it wasn't—it exceeded our stamina, however, by a good 180 square feet. We then peeled back the sod in a 9-foot by 3-foot patch. It took over two hours. Both of us were up to our elbows in mud, brandishing steak knives like crazy folk, slashing at the roots with desperation and dismay. Then, with his and her shovels and a large scrap of heavy-duty plastic, we struggled to haul our sod from the garden to the grub farm.

Sod is hugely heavy when you leave 5 inches of dirt attached. Still, we managed to move it in only three trips—three difficult, muscle-wrenching, silent trips. I could tell that my sweaty and dirt-streaked husband was not having a good time. Because when he is unhappy, he becomes politely aloof and definitely tight-lipped. And he tends to gaze skyward a lot. After three loads of sod, he looked like he was communing with St. Peter himself.

Before we could plant our new baby shrubs, we realized we had to fluff up their bed. The area looked lumpy and bare and badly in need of some extra soil. A dirt-run to the home improvement center was in order. And we looked like bums. Really. My husband's knees were caked with mud, and his sweatshirt was spotted and grimy. I looked about the same, but I had more layers, including a fleece under my long-sleeved, white, tick-detecting T-shirt. Sweating, I peeled off the shirt and suddenly looked a whole lot cleaner. Had husband done the same, he would have been down to his underwear.

"I thought we weren't going to change," he groused as he pulled the car keys from his pocket, ready to head to the store.

Ten minutes later, we were at our local Walmart. I did the choosing and my husband did the heavy lifting. I selected three bags of garden soil—aka, manure—seeding soil and a handful of household items.

In no time we were back at the ranch, digging holes, mixing soil, splaying roots and leveling plants. We spread dirt and seed among the upstart clods of sod for at least an hour more. My guy was a real trooper, but a tired one. He spent the last 15 minutes on his belly, spreading dirt with his fingertips. Fragrant and filthy, it was an OxiClean moment, for sure.

After five hours of labor, the garden looked great, even if

it smelled like a dairy farm. The plants had plenty of breathing room, and the bed looked clean and tidy. Even my husband was pleased with the results.

"It was worth the effort," he announced. Then he quickly added, "How about a drink?"

Turns out, this DIY project had tested both our gardening skills and our partnering skills. I'd give us a blue ribbon for our efforts all round. Plus, I learned that in "Paradise," you have to spend money to save money. Save a little, spend a lot. That seems to be the DIY rule.

Dead grubs and the finished garden

# Teamwork

by
Alice Muschany

While riding my bike along the Missouri Katy Trail, I spotted a picturesque flower garden edged with brick. Hopping off my bike, I grabbed my Nikon and snapped away. For the rest of my ride, I visualized turning my yard into a showplace that would put the White House to shame.

Once back home, I rushed inside to tell my husband, Roland, my great idea.

Funny, he seemed less enthused.

To my delight, though, the following week, Roland hauled home a load of bricks, enough to remodel a Hilton. He then began the strenuous project of making his lovely wife a flower bed to die for.

First he measured a 4-foot-wide path in a huge circle. Then he spent the rest of the hot August afternoon digging out the area and removing grass and excess dirt.

The next morning, Roland poured sand onto the path before beginning the back-breaking task of placing bricks in the exact same pattern as in the photo. My job consisted of delivering iced tea and encouraging him with comments like, "We're almost halfway done."

By late afternoon, the beverage switched to Bud Lite. After all, I had to make sure my worker didn't walk off the job.

On day three, Roland swept sand between the bricks to hold them in place. The completed flower bed looked even better than the one it was designed after. Perhaps I should have waited a smidge before announcing, "With all that leftover brick, we could make a pathway connecting the front sidewalks."

Too tired to answer, he just shrugged. But the next morning, my persevering husband crawled out of bed and began the procedure all over again—removing dirt, spreading sand, and laying brick for the extended walkway. This time, I bragged even more about how awesome it looked and began serving him an ice cold one before church was out. Thank goodness the path was shorter.

Roland glanced at the stack behind him that hadn't diminished much and mumbled a few swear words.

"Pardon me. Are you complaining?"

"No darling. I just said we should've bricked the house instead."

While he slaved away, I let my imagination run wild. "I can see it now—row after row of kaleidoscope tulips in my gigantic flower bed and fragrant daffodils bordering the walk and blowing in the warm southern breeze."

When he reminded me balmy weather was a long way off, I replied, "A gal can dream, can't she?"

Sighing, he said, "Sounds like a nightmare to me. Who's gonna plant all those bulbs?"

"We are, sweetie."

When Roland finished, once again I raved about how great it looked. And once again in a flash of genius, it occurred to me perhaps we should replace the old, cracked sidewalks in front of the house. Just then, he stood and stretched his aching back. I thought about making another beer run before announcing my latest brainstorm, but decided now wasn't a good time to bring it up.

The next day, I walked over and stood on the sunken sidewalks, glancing back and forth at the new brick path. Roland must've had ESP because I heard him moan before trudging out to the shed and grabbing a sledge hammer. He chipped away at the existing 10-inch-thick concrete that had most likely been there since the 60-year-old clapboard house was built. My husband finally placed the last brick and announced, "There's not enough left for anything else."

Kind of sounded like a warning. I nodded in agreement.

After hours of blood, sweat and tears, half our yard was bricked. Our neighbor walked over to view the masterpiece and went on and on about how fantastic it looked.

Later, I said to my exhausted husband, "We did a great job, didn't we?"

"What's with the 'we' stuff? I only recall one of us doing the manual labor."

I grinned and put my arms around him, "Honey, know

what we need to replace next?"

Without skipping a beat, he replied, "You. That is, if you think of any more projects 'we' need to work on."

The completed brickwork

# Letting Go

by
Tori Nichols

"Hire somebody? Why? We can do this!"

With the utterance of those exact words, I had sealed my own fate.

A procession of fence posts and boards waited in an outline along the ground. They stretched from the driveway entry down the hill to the creek, all told, the impressive length of a football field. Bids for professional installation had been staggering. We'd had a brief, but successful history as proud do-it-yourselfers. Surely a simple fence couldn't intimidate us.

I took my part in the upcoming adventure seriously. My husband was counting on me. After all, the girl he married was a strong, independent woman who tackled challenges head-on. I had no intention of changing his opinion of me now. Discredit my reputation? Disappoint him? Never! I would not fail. My word was my bond, my promise. Like a marital vow, for better or worse, I would see the project through to its end.

Having made that commitment, I was eager to get started—the posts weren't going to set themselves. Victory always depends on having the right tool for the job, so one quick trip into town and we would be outfitted for the first step, the burrowing of postholes.

The two of us stood outside the entrance to the most comprehensive tool rental store in our area. Two stories of gray concrete blocks loomed hard and austere above us. It struck me as being not unlike the medieval castles of old. The walk to the sales counter was oddly like a gauntlet flanked with every size and shape of blades, drills, clamps and saws one could imagine. My husband spoke with the gentleman on duty and conveyed our project plan. The clerk's eyes panned across the room and he pointed a finger to the far corner.

"Back there's the model you need," he instructed.

Against the wall leaned the technology that was going to help us get the job done—an ominous machine with an engine-head painted in blood-red and a dragon-like twisting tail blade of sharp, shining silver that looked as though it could drill to China if the task so required. Two sets of cold steel bars protruding from its chest were all that hinted at the taming of a beast. The clerk called it a two-man, gas-powered, corkscrew earth auger.

I remarked, rather disrespectfully, "Fancy name for a posthole digger, don't you think?"

I would later learn of some world religions that teach when one disrespects the spirit of even inanimate objects, the irreverence will bring negative energy. Unfortunately, this was a multicultural lesson that came too late for me.

"Show no fear!" That was the motto of the valiant knights.

So, with a swagger in my step, I approached this modern drag-on, emanating all the self-confidence I could muster. My foe was nearly as tall as me and weighed as much. Threatening, yes, but I remained undaunted.

The clerk glared at me with a raised, questioning eyebrow. "Lot of power in this here baby. You gotta hold on tight, little lady. Think you can handle it?"

Annoyed by the implication of inabilities of the fairer gender, I uttered a restrained, "Sure." But the silent voice of my cocky ego said, *Bring it on!*

Back at home, the project got underway. An operating manual lay on the ground, unread. After all, the process seemed pretty straightforward to me: apply pressure, dig hole, lift. I admit the vibrations were stronger than I anticipated, but muscle and determination would prevail. Together, with each of us in charge of an opposing set of handlebars, we managed to create several perfect postholes.

Everything was going so smoothly that I was feeling triumphant. *Conquered another dragon*, I thought. That notion no sooner registered in my brain when the voice of the dragon changed its tone, unmistakably deeper, almost angry. The motor was stalling, the blade decelerating. "Trouble" has a feeling, and this was it.

We'd hit a large tree root and the blade locked. Two bodies stiffened and four eyeballs widened instantaneously! My deficient study of the manual had left me unprepared for this specific scenario. *What should I do?* All I could hear in my head was the clerk's warning, *You gotta hold on tight, little lady.* And that's exactly what I did. My willful personality took over and I squeezed those handlebars with 10 white knuckles, resolving not to let go, no matter what!

Unfortunately, my husband responded on pure instinct. Assuming I would do likewise, he let go and stepped back. He knew about the automatic kill switch that activates whenever hands disengage from the grips. I'll give you one guess who didn't even know what a "kill switch" was.

Within a nanosecond, I was flying. I could go into the *Guinness Book of World Records* listed under fastest, tightest, circular human flight in history. Two revolutions—that's how long it's possible to hang on before centrifugal force spins you into space. And when that happened, I was airborne, completely unaided and sailing like a bird. I had time for three thoughts:

1. *How fast am I traveling over this green-grass blur?*
2. *Why do I hear my husband laughing at a time like this?*
3. *Tuck and roll! Tuck and roll!*

Luckily, there was a happy ending. I was bruised, bumped and sore all over, but nothing was broken, except a bit of pride. The fence was eventually finished and in the aftermath, I gave myself an "A" for effort, plus a stern sermon. Since that incident, I do my homework, learning absolutely everything I can about the equipment I will be using. Knowledge is power. I now have a healthy respect for all life's dragons and steer clear of negative energy.

They say what doesn't kill you makes you stronger. I'm feeling pretty strong these days.

# CHAPTER NINE

# Women Who Get'r Done

Girls gone wild . . . with tools!

# I Can Do Anything

by
## Bobby Barbara Smith

My plans to remodel my master bedroom were instantly rejected.

"You can't do that by yourself—that's a two-man job," my brother-in-law said, stopping short of speaking what his face revealed. "This is not a job for a woman, never mind a woman who has never operated a jigsaw or caulk gun."

Having just gone through a divorce, I was experiencing a feeling of freedom and an urge to declare it. No man was going to stop me, not even my concerned brother-in-law. For years I had longed to redo my bedroom. Now, I could make my own decisions. And I decided that now was the time.

"I can do this!" I snapped at my brother-in-law, wishing I hadn't opened my big fat mouth in the first place. But apparently he had seen the same determination in the past from his wife—my sister—and rapidly changed his tune.

"I'm just saying, it's a difficult room, what with the slanted ceiling and that little octagon window. It would be difficult for me. You'll need to make a template for the window and the electrical outlets. Do you know how to do that?" He wasn't winning any points. The Missouri mule in me came out bucking and snorting.

"I've done that for the kid's costumes—it can't be much different." I gave him my most confidant stare, but inside doubt was building.

"You're going to need help holding the 8-foot pieces while nailing them," he warned, and then graciously offered his assistance with the project if I could wait until he had some time off from work.

I didn't want to wait. I'd waited way too long as it was. I didn't want his help, but I thanked him for the offer and promised to call if I ran into a problem.

Red and black were the "in" colors in the 1970s for the bold and daring, and that's exactly how I was feeling. After a shopping trip to my local home improvement store, I settled on a smoky wood-grain paneling with red carpet. I purchased black paint for the baseboards and sliding closet doors. I also found an ornate swag light fixture to replace the ugly light bulb sticking out of the wall above my bed.

I couldn't start the project until I had a day off from work—I just couldn't wait. Finally, when the day arrived, my first task was to remove the baseboards, facings and closet doors. This went well, fueling my confidence and newfound power. I even vented about my divorce by painting words of defiance in black paint on the white drywall. It was so cathartic to paint those words, words and a former life I would cover up with the paneling. But then it occurred to me that the children would be home from school before I got to the paneling, so I quickly painted over my liberating words.

The next few days at my job were torture, as I wanted nothing more than to get back to my project. Counting the days, I was filled with anticipation and a healthy amount of trepidation.

Back on my DIY project, I measured my first piece of paneling and cut it. I placed it in the corner and it fit.

"Yes!" I felt proud as I removed it and armed myself with the caulk gun, which was loaded with construction adhesive.

My brother-in-law's words of warning flashed through my head. *Once that glue grabs, you can't get it off, so make sure your edges are lined up.* I shrugged off his advice, applied the glue and held my breath as I carefully lined up the edge before pressing the first sheet of paneling into place. It fit like a glove and I nailed it in securely. The next few pieces went smoothly as I measured, cut, glued and nailed my way around the light fixture, an electrical plug outlet and the closet doors.

I have to say, I was feeling downright cocky. I burst into renditions of *I Am Woman*. Helen Reddy and I had it going on.

Next, I squared off and looked at the octagon-shaped window. Then, with template in hand, I marked the paneling and made my first cut.

"Just look at that perfect cut," I purred as I nailed the paneling into place.

Then I made the second cut. *What the hell?* I lamented to myself, fitful over a tiny quarter-inch gap at one of the corners when I put the paneling into place. I tried to move the facing over to cover it, but that was worse.

*Well, crap.* I had been doing so well. *How did this happen?*

Once again, more advice from my brother-in-law surfaced in my brain: *It wouldn't hurt to buy an extra piece or even two in case you need to re-cut one.*

To that piece of advice, I had smugly replied, "I won't. I'll be fine." I barely had enough money as it was, so buying extra paneling was not an option.

I stood back and looked at the tiny gap and decided black paint on the wall behind would hide my one flaw—and it did. But I vowed to be more careful on the remaining cuts.

My sister and brother-in-law dropped by as I was finishing up for the day, and I watched with bated breath as they surveyed my work. I could see a look of surprise on my brother-in-law's face. My sister was amazed and proud. They didn't even notice my flawed corner until I pointed it out.

I just needed one more day to finish the project. I went to sleep that night exhausted, but anxious. The next morning, armed with fresh coffee and a determination to complete my bedroom remodel, I went to work. I made my way around the double window and down to the last piece of paneling. All I needed to do was to cut it lengthwise to fit and make one cut around the last electrical outlet. I measured and marked the piece, and then decided to take a break before cutting it.

Two phone calls later, kids now home from school and with supper on the stove, I returned to my project.

I zipped down the vertical line with my saw, slapped on the glue and after checking the top and inside edge, I pressed the panel into place, working my way toward the bottom.

*Oh, my God.* My hand felt a bulge under the paneling, and my heart sank as I realized what I'd done. *I forgot to cut out the electric outlet!* I grabbed the free corner and tried to pull the paneling off. It wouldn't budge. That's when I knew I had to make the call of shame. With crow feathers flying from my mouth, I confessed over the phone to my brother-in-law that I needed his help. I was so close. I was on the last piece and I could have claimed victory, if not for this one mistake.

I set in a puddle of defeat as I watched my brother-in-law carefully punching out the outlet.

"You'll need to get a bigger plate, but that should work," he helpfully suggested.

The last piece snapped into place and I breathed a sigh of relief.

After he left, I knew what I had to do. I had to reclaim my dignity, and I knew just how to do it. I would feed the kids then tackle the mounting of my new swag light fixture.

I laid out all the parts, read through the instructions twice and turned off the main power. Then I picked up my screwdriver, opened up the old light, paying close attention to the order of connection. My plan was to backtrack, using the same connections. I didn't have a clue what I was doing and was surprised when I finished the job so quickly. I admired the new light fixture for a while, dreading the true test. I had to turn the power back on.

I made a mental plan of escape before I hit the breaker. I flipped it and listened. I didn't hear any frying sounds or see sparks coming from the breaker box. *So far, so good.*

I made my way back to the bedroom and faced the final moment of truth—flipping on the light switch. I reached for it much like I would reach for a rattlesnake, leery and prepared to run for my life.

Using one finger, I flipped the switch. Suddenly, beautiful light flooded the room, without so much as a hiss or a sputter. I stood there in awe, gazing at my masterpiece. I couldn't wait to show my sister and brother-in-law. Yes, I felt vindicated. I whirled around to glare at that last piece of paneling and hateful electrical outlet, both nemeses in my effort to prove I could complete the entire project myself.

"Take that!" I boasted proudly to the two inanimate objects. My kids came rushing in to see who would dare cross their mother, but were instantly distracted by the new masterpiece hanging over the bed. I basked in the glory as they proclaimed me "Super Mom!"

Bobby's ready to work!

A few months later, when I took a job in a different town, the one thing I hated to leave was my bedroom. The house sold quickly and when the realtor told me it was the bedroom that did the trick, I laughed all the way to the bank.

Days later, packed and ready for our move, I closed the door to my house and drove off toward a new beginning—just me, the children, the cat and Helen Reddy singing the soundtrack to my life.

# Bait Me

by
## Pat Nelson

I had been living in a war zone for more than eight weeks. The steady coming and going of determined infantrymen had affected my sanity. I couldn't shut my eyes to sleep without dreaming of soldiers marching out of my pillowcase, across my extended arm and up the wall before streaming across the ceiling in a continuous line. Night after night, they invaded my sleep. Day after day, they invaded my kitchen, my study, my walk-in closet and my bathroom.

"You can't deal with this yourself," said my husband, Bob, raising his eyebrows and jutting his chin forward to create that "duh" look.

"Sure I can," I replied with Norwegian stubbornness. "Exterminators are expensive. I'm not giving them one cent of our vacation money."

"Well, don't be so thrifty that you let the little creatures destroy our home!" he said as he turned and walked out the door. The door said *thump* a little too loudly.

Determined to take care of the home invaders myself, I weighed my options. *I could gas them*, I thought. *I could set out traps. I could use brute force. I could consult the Internet and become an expert.* I sat at my computer researching, printing pages and highlighting the information that might solve my problem. Finally, I had a plan.

I pulled a jar of peanut butter from the cupboard and put a large scoop of the creamy delight into a yellow plastic margarine tub. Next, I added a generous portion of maple syrup, the good stuff brought home from a trip to Canada. I stirred the mixture well and dipped a finger into it for a taste test before adding the secret ingredient—a double dose of lethal boric acid. I stirred until the poison disappeared. Even with the added toxin, the smooth, creamy mixture smelled like the candy shop at the mall.

I searched the garage until I found the masking tape—not the skinny stuff, but a wide roll. I tore off foot-long strips and stuck them to my kitchen counter. Scooping up a gob of the tan cream, I spread it onto the masking tape, and then covered another piece, and another, as though I were preparing sandwiches for a crowd. I carefully picked up each piece and stuck it tightly to the floor tiles in the areas where the armies had been observed. I would not allow these warriors to attack my home and turn it to powdery sawdust.

As I washed my hands, the phone rang. It was Bob. "Meet me for lunch at Los Pepes," he said. "You're probably tired of fighting your invaders."

It felt good to enjoy a relaxing meal away from the raging war going on inside our home. An hour later, I walked back through the door singing my own words to the tune of the *Pink Panther*, "Dead ant, dead ant . . . dead ant, dead ant, dead ant."

I checked a strip of the tape. Infantrymen lined up in a row across it, methodically devouring the sticky goo. A few hours later, they had completely cleaned a piece of tape, leaving no trace of the peanut butter poison bait. I felt victorious.

I re-spread the mixture onto the tape, and the ants kept arriving, and arriving, and arriving. Finally, with mass ant death nowhere to be seen, I admitted that the only thing I had accomplished was to focus their attention on certain areas so that I no longer found them marching across my kitchen counters and crawling out of my computer keyboard.

One evening, when our six-year-old granddaughter was spending the night with us, a friend of mine stopped by to visit. She had just read that ants would not cross a line of chalk. Our granddaughter ran to her room and grabbed a stick. She carefully drew a horseshoe-shaped line on the floor tile from the baseboard, around a group of ants, and back to the baseboard on the other side. A couple of ants brazenly crossed the narrow chalk line. She drew the line thicker. One ant tried to cross, but only got to the center of the line before turning back. It had worked! We had found a way to corral the little pests. As we gloated about our success, some of the ants changed directions. They climbed up the baseboard then up the wall, smartly escaping from their chalk-line fence.

A few days later, when ants emerged in a new location, Bob convinced me that it was time to admit defeat. Not willing to spend money on an exterminator and still wanting to do it myself, I grabbed a can of ant spray and went to work. When I had thoroughly sprayed the little soldiers, we opened windows and doors and left the house while the poison worked its magic. This time when we returned, I could truly sing, "Dead ant, dead ant . . . dead ant, dead ant, dead ant."

The next day, our neighbor knocked on the patio door. "Do you have any more of that peanut-butter concoction for the ants?" he asked. "I don't know what happened, but our house is infested with them this morning."

"Sure," I said, handing him the yellow tub of sticky-sweet poison. "I don't need it anymore."

Pat mixing her creamy ant poison

# The Mystery Machine

by
## Jill Pertler

Normally I'd call a professional repairperson to fix a major appliance. It's the prudent thing to do.

Then again, no one's ever described me as prudent.

The problem with my fridge started out small—a drip here, a pitter-patter there. My first reaction was that of any normal person. I ignored the situation. You know, like one ignores a squeaky step, leaky faucet or any birthday after age 40. I sort of got used to the drip and forgot it existed.

Then the problem grew. Water trickled out of the freezer compartment and down into the fridge with increasing frequency. I placed a cup under the leak and went about my business. Remember, ignorance is bliss.

This wasn't a perfect solution. Sometimes, the cup would tip over. Or I'd forget to empty it and the water would pour all over the fridge. As I wiped up the wet mess, I grumbled about the inferiority of my appliance.

Since my freezer wasn't equipped with an automatic ice-maker, the situation was quite mysterious. I'm no Scooby or Shaggy, but I've always enjoyed a good mystery. Besides, I figured maybe I had a big problem on my hands. Maybe my fridge was dying. Maybe I'd end up with a brand-new one. I was thinking stainless steel, with an icemaker, maybe a side-by-side. Prudent or not, a girl can dream.

Deciding to be like Thelma on *Scooby-Doo!*, I researched the problem. I went online and Googled "freezer leaking water" and discovered that many people had experienced the same thing with their refrigerators. Best of all, they gave detailed instructions on how to fix the problem.

I have never been one to ignore detailed instructions. They call out to me like a Scooby Snack. Within seconds, I was searching for something called a "drain pan."

I didn't know a drain pan from the Mystery Machine, but I wasn't going to let a detail like that stop me. I emptied the freezer and thought I was pretty sure I had positively identified the drain pan. It was a plastic thing at the bottom of the freezer that looked decidedly . . . well . . . pan-like.

The instructions said to remove the pan. Trouble was, the metal doohickeys that attached the pan to the freezer were situated within a concave dimple of plastic and I didn't know how to reach them.

Not to be thwarted, I called my husband and described the problem. He introduced me to two new vocabulary words: "socket" and "ratchet." Turns out these were important tools he had hidden in a tool box in the basement. I wonder what else he had down there.

I learned that the socket fits on top of a nut. Or is it a bolt?

The ratchet doohickey connects to the socket and turns the nut. I got a socket to fit, but despite my husband's patient and flawless over-the-phone directives, I couldn't ratchet to save my life. "Jinkies," as Thelma would say. My nuts were stuck.

Lucky for me, there was a screwdriver implement that also attached to the socket. To qualify my credentials as a do-it-yourselfer, I am nearly a professional when it comes to screwdrivers and can distinguish a "slotted" from a "Phillips" with a high amount of accuracy. In this case, I needed a Phillips.

I removed the nuts and sure enough, my drain pan was sitting on a glacier. It was clear my drain was iced over and clogged. The water created during the automatic defrost cycle of the freezer had nowhere to go but down into my fridge. Problem solved. Give this girl a Scooby Snack!

My fridge was saved. I wasn't sure if that was good news or not. I guess I won't be getting the stainless steel model any time

soon. Still, I must have saved some money on what a professional repair would cost. I could probably charge about $75 an hour for my expert services. Problem is, I'd have to bill myself.

Except that would not be prudent, now, would it?

Jill and the Mystery Machine

# Up Against a Brick Wall

by
## Suzanne Olsen

I couldn't help myself. I was literally up against a wall. A pinkish brick wall, ugly as a plucked parrot and one of the last remodeling projects we needed to do on our 1950's fixer-upper.

I take pride in my home. It looked good except outside where there was an old, curved feature wall that held four large cedar trees and assorted landscape plants on the driveway end. As a domestic engineer, I had to do something.

When I asked my husband if we could finally tackle the wall, he said, "Let's wait until we replace the cracked driveway. Then we'll rip them both out at the same time."

"When's that going to be?" I asked.

"In about five years."

"Why do we have to wait so long?" I wailed, but it made perfect sense and I resolved to be patient.

That lasted about a month. Every time I drove into the driveway, which was about 80 times a day, that wall spoke to me, and it wasn't very nice. "I get to be pink and ugly for 59 more months, and you can't do a single thing about it." I felt like it was sticking its pink tongue out at me and sometimes even adding the word, "Bitch!"

I started rationalizing that it was in my family's best interest for me to do something right now. Not anything as drastic as tearing down the wall, but something cosmetic to get rid of the pink. Before long I had an idea, and shortly after that, a plan. I would proceed without mentioning anything to my husband.

Let me explain why I have to hide my projects from him. My husband has reason to believe that once I start a project, it will take way longer than I anticipated and everything else will be neglected. This includes our children, meals, laundry and late-night activities. To avoid marital conflict, I've learned it's best to let my husband in on my projects at a more diplomatic time, generally after they are beyond the point of no return.

The do-it-yourself books I checked out of the library about applying stucco made it seem pretty easy. Stucco, at least the kind they described, is simply water combined with mortar mix, the stuff that contractors use when they're laying tile. It's basically concrete without the rocks.

I have mixed concrete before, and it was a real pain for me to get it smooth because some of the rocks were the size of Italy. But mortar mix would be a piece of cake. I could trowel it over the pink bricks and create a nice, smooth surface on them like I'd seen on those homes in Palm Springs. Better still, it would be a classy, natural gray that would go with the color of the house.

I bought several bags of mortar mix at Home Depot and hid them in the tool shed. After my husband left for work the next morning, I hoisted a bag of mortar into a wheelbarrow and added water. I mixed it with a shovel and thought to myself, *This is a whole lot like mixing concrete, and surprisingly just as miserable, even without those pesky rocks.* I should have stopped right then and there.

When I dipped into the soft mortar mix and went to smooth it onto the wall, it slid off the trowel like butter on a stack of steaming pancakes, splattering onto the blacktop driveway. "Son of a . . . !" I shouted. I couldn't say the whole thing because my young daughter was playing close by.

When I tried to get the mess up, I realized it had seeped into the millions of little holes and crevices inherent in cracked blacktop. I scraped up what I could then hosed off the rest. I sprayed it all the way down to the street so it wouldn't leave a permanent grayish-white layer on top of the driveway. This took so long that the mortar mix in the wheelbarrow was getting thicker and starting to harden.

I read that you're not supposed to add more water to mortar once it's mixed because it weakens it, so I had to scramble to use it before it got any worse. I grabbed a plastic painter's tarp, putting it on the blacktop to catch any further drips, and proceeded to get about 30 percent of my trowel loads of mortar onto the wall. The remaining 70 percent formed a polka-dot pattern of gray blobs on the tarp.

As the mortar got thicker, it didn't want to cling to the brick wall. In fact, it was like those magnets that oppose each other. If I managed to magically get it from the wheelbarrow to the brick, it would spring off the wall and plop onto the tarp.

I was able to cover about two feet of wall with lumpy mortar that wouldn't level out with the trowel. Some of the lumps were so big they cast shadows. I put on gloves and tried to beat them down with my fist. Then I smoothed them as best I could by pressing and rubbing them with all my might. Luckily, that part of the wall was by the side of the house, so it wasn't visible from the street.

Cleanup was a nightmare. I had to chisel hardened mortar off the trowel, and then scrub the wheelbarrow and shovel with a stiff brush. The painter's tarp was almost as heavy as the original bag of mortar mix. All the bending and squatting to apply the mortar to the low wall made every inch of my body sore, except the top of my head, which soon developed a headache.

When my husband came home from work that evening, he didn't notice the project I'd started. I figured once I got around to the front, I'd be more experienced and he'd see how nice it looked and be thrilled, especially since it was such an inexpensive way to make the house attractive for the next five years.

I hadn't counted on having to pretend my body wasn't aching. I lacked energy and compulsively reapplied lotion to my rough, red hands. When he asked what was wrong, I told him I had a headache, which was absolutely true.

The next morning, I arose feeling even stiffer than the night before. I'd gotten smarter overnight, though. Before starting again, I covered my hands with a thick coat of lotion and to keep them from getting so irritated, I put them in sandwich bags then slipped on a pair of gloves. I used a plastic garbage bag in the wheelbarrow and mixed the mortar in that. I could add the water and knead it around in the bag instead of having to dirty up the shovel, and it kept the wheelbarrow clean. I put my tarp down before I started. Plus, I decided to hell with the trowel and grabbed fistfuls of mortar, slapping the mixture onto the wall then rubbing it with my palms.

I was able to slap mortar on about four more feet of wall and got it somewhat smoother than with the trowel. It now looked like rolling hills in Texas. My innovations made the process easier, but without diminishing any of the pain and suffering. I ached more than the day before, though I couldn't believe that was possible. With 60 feet of the wall still to go, I started calculating and figured I'd be finished in—I had to choke back tears—15 more days! I didn't even want to do one more day. I thought I'd be finished by now!

I couldn't say anything to my husband, because I knew he'd pitch a fit. If he had to hire someone to finish the job, it would cost a wheelbarrow full of money, not to mention my injured pride. Nope. I had to see it through. I had to fake being energetic. I had to cook and clean and do laundry. I had to pay attention to my children.

My can-do attitude lasted one more day. At the end of day three, my work was visible from the street. When my husband got out of the car, he caught me cleaning up for the day. He stood with his hands on his hips, mouth wide open and slowly shook his head.

"What in the hell have you done?" he asked.

"I'm covering up these ugly pink bricks. Doesn't it look good?"

"It does, but what a mess."

"There isn't any mess," I protested. "I've cleaned everything up. See how this wheelbarrow sparkles?"

"You're the mess," he said. "This explains the headaches and going to bed early. I should have known."

He walked into the house still shaking his head. I imagined he was thinking that I had bitten off more than I could chew—again—and I wouldn't admit it. He knew from experience that I'd get it finished one way or another and everyone else would be miserable until it was done.

As usual, he was right. It took me every bit of 15 days and then some. I ached every single day. Squatting and bending and rubbing the wall mechanically back and forth for several hours at a time never got any easier. The laundry piled up, my husband had to get dinner on the table, my fair-skinned daughter got sunburned from playing outside while I worked and I fell sound asleep immediately after the kids went down.

When the new and improved wall was finished, it looked pretty good, but not quite like the houses in Palm Springs. We eventually redid the driveway, and I was surprised my husband wanted to leave the wall. I figured he would replace it with some pretty stonework. But I think he wanted to leave it to remind me not to ever do anything that stupid again.

I wish I could say that it worked.

The old wall (above) and the new wall (below)

# GDCS

by
## Susan Swartwout

I try to recycle everything—and I mean everything. Therefore, the trash collectors hate me. They attach scores of red warning stickers to my recycling container. Despite the formal warnings, I know what they really want to say is, "Read the guidelines. You're nuts, lady. What part of food contamination do you not understand?" I've wasted chunks of my life dragging my rejected trash back from the curb—time I could have used doing something important like putting comments on Facebook or my favorite crime blog.

In light of the complaint stickers, I've been forced to consider alternative uses for the detritus of modern life that isn't on the Approved Recycling List. Consider, as an example, the set of undersized, pink gardening tools that my niece and her husband sent me on my birthday. These little impotent garden tools are bigger than Barbie-sized, but smaller than child-sized, with metallic paint and plastic handles with no triangular recycling symbol. Putting these in the recycling bin would incite the city collectors to bring a WMD (Warning of Major Disapproval) to my home.

This dilemma plagued me for months. The tiny tools could be artistically displayed in a houseplant pot, with their handles crossed for luck, but that was a short-term fix. Maybe I could tie them onto a birthday present, leaving their fate to another celebrant instead of me. Possibly, I could stab them upright into my neighbor's plastic-flowered window box as retaliation for the hideous, environmentally irresponsible concrete slab she recently installed. She calls it her "outdoor kitchen." It's a damn slab. On the slab she positioned a grill, two plastic Lifesavers-candy-colored, un-recyclable Adirondack chairs and an upside-down bucket for an end table, all geometrically aligned, all as anti-nature as Rush Limbaugh.

I know how to call a slab a slab. I'm less sure how to make my utter-crap toy tools into anything remotely useful. I'm frozen with eco-guilt and it's all my parents' fault. They were born during the Great Depression, the precursor to this excess generation's Ronco Veg-o-Matic success. I'm a victim of Mom and Dad's "Great Depression Consumerism Syndrome." Also known as GDCS, it is an inquisitional disease that attacks the brain at either an object's "Point of Purchase" or at the object's "Moment of Riddance."

Let me explain. If you find yourself slack-jawed in Walmart in front of a tufa stone statue of Cupid poignantly holding out a tufa flower, you are a victim of GDCS at Point of Purchase.

I was stricken with a terrible bout of GDCS when I found myself thinking how nice that tufa Cupid would look next to the marigolds. I really needed a focal point to draw the eye away from the rotting wooden fence and the grass-bare back-yard. I was thinking how this adorable fat cupid symbolized that giving is better than receiving, and how my family's lives would be enriched by the fine art of symbolism.

Five minutes later, he was in the bright orange Walmart cart and I was pushing him toward checkout. I'd come to buy groceries, but there was no longer room in the cart for food. As a side effect of my severe case of GDCS, I effectively blot-ted out every logical detractor that questioned my decision to pay $29.99 for this *objet d'art*. I am not deterred by my lim-ited budget or total uselessness of the object, because I have a higher purpose—making do with an immediately available aesthetic crutch.

A year later, my weather-beaten Cupid didn't seem like such a good idea. He had mismanaged his tufa fig leaf. His crotch-covering was listing at such an angle that it could have easily been mistaken for a desire to "know" the neighbors better. Cupid also enriched our lives when our grandson brought his giggling friends over at an alarmingly increased rate. It was then that I was forced to succumb to the GDCS Moment of Riddance.

I could completely dispose of the horny cherub, believing whole-heartedly that a hammer is always excellent therapy. Or I could explore the possibilities inherent in making do with him in other ways. I am a Make-do Mama, so I choose creativity.

The fig leaf, completely removed, was decoratively glued to the tool shed's wall. The pedestal—leaving Cupid's legs in-tact to give it more heft—now serves as a shed door holder, since the door only has one hinge.

But wait—there's more! Cupid's head, sans neck, was artistically placed in the hollyhock patch, as if it were a stone that had fallen there naturally. But—oh, look!—what a delightful surprise; it's actually a severed head. Yes, I have a head in my garden that is not lettuce or cabbage. It's an art head.

I know that recycling those annoying unrecyclables is a noble task. So when a GDCS Moment of Riddance strikes, I have to ask myself three questions:

1. Do I really love this object? If no, go to #2;
2. Does it have a valid recycling symbol printed on it? If no, go to #3;
3. Will it enhance my life if I render it into art/furniture/puppets/placeholders, and will it not completely piss off the neighbors?"

As literary critic Viktor Shklovsky said, "Art is the object as seen, not recognized." However, if the unrecyclable is a gift from a family member, reevaluate your relationship. It may be time to change your will or enter a protection program similar to the ones they have to protect witnesses.

Cupid, pre-recycled

# Even if Askew

by
Janet Sheppard Kelleher

Today was the day. I would attempt a job that was apparently at the bottom of my husband's honey-do list—attach a mirror to its dresser.

With sheer determination, I single-handedly brought that commodious mirror down from the attic, which had been its home since we moved in 12 long years ago. The dresser was in the spare room, and I smiled over the fact that this humongous reflector would satisfy even the most narcissistic of our guests.

My friend Merrie came over to help me. We shined the wood up nicely with Pledge and the glass with Windex. Then we laid the mirror on the guestroom bed as I thought through the task and scrutinized the most efficient way of proceeding. Senior-citizen women should always wade through a problem in their minds before they expend needless energy with the weight of the project in their hands.

Not applying that plan of attack leads to what the old folks call being "stove up."

I determined the way we were going to tackle the problem and what tools were needed: a Phillips screwdriver and a few 1-3/4-inch wood screws. I bolted to the basement where hubby keeps the handyman accoutrements to look for the perfect screw. It was as elusive as its double entendre. I finally found one screw the exact size I needed and brought up three more that could possibly work. They absolutely did not.

Then, on a lark, I looked in my desk. What? Sometimes loose screws end up in one of those little sections made for paper clips or rubber bands, right? There I found another fairly decent, although thinner, screw. So after testing it also, I summed up the situation: I had one perfect screw and one loose screw.

Not enough. I needed two more screws. Desperately!

*Aha!* I remembered I'd just taken the air conditioner out of my upstairs office window and recalled where I had put the screws that held it in place. Trouble is, I knew they were considerably shorter, but thought they could be the right width. And they were wood screws, which is what I needed.

I bounded to my home office and grabbed those screws. Then, and only then, after we had all pieces of the puzzle assembled and within reach, Merrie and I lifted the mirror to its proper position on top of the dresser.

While screwing fast and furiously, I figured if I put the thin screw in sort of catawampus, it would work just fine. And it did. Like Lady MacBeth said, "Screw your courage to the sticking place, and we'll not fail." Success! Each little threaded piece of iron went in like, well, um, like a good screw does and held everything in place without the use of our hands!

So, the way I see it, I have to agree with the guys about this one thing: Size doesn't matter, just as long as it goes in easy, isn't too long and gets the job done!

Janet and Merrie just screwing around

# It's All Good

by
## Sally Fingerett

Once the moving van left, my 10-year-old daughter E.J. and I crossed the threshold of our new, but used, 70-year-old house. School had just ended for the summer and there was furniture to arrange, closets to fill, drawers to organize, a kitchen to stock and, of course, some good old-fashioned mother and daughter fighting in case we veered off task.

It was going to be just the two of us now, sharing ideas on how to decorate. She wanted to live in a dollhouse; I wanted to keep the pink under control. We worked hard each day and after a quick dinner, we'd fly outdoors to make new friends. E.J. would monkey around with her sidewalk chalk, I sat in a lawn chair immobilized with overwhelming exhaustion and the stunning realization that being the sole owner of this house was going to be a fairly significant gig.

Within a few shorts days, my happy-go-lucky daughter

slid right in with the kids on the block. Watching her go, I found myself sucked into a vortex of anxiety and became obsessed with yardwork. I trimmed the bushes too low, killed the grass and accidentally dug up the roots of lily bulbs. But in spite of all this, I adored being outside and soon made friends on the block, too. These kind folks found my lawn care mistakes charming and offered tremendous support. They generously lent me everything from hoses and sprinklers to weedwhackers and shovels.

My girlfriends surprised me with housewarming/divorce gifts—tools from the Sears Craftsmen Collection. Unlike some gals, I am not a woman with a closet full of shoes, but rather, a single mom with tools. I loved my presents and not just because they were shiny and new, but because these possessions gave me independence, which that first summer, was also shiny and new.

My girlfriends' assurance that I can do anything gave me a raging case of can-do and I took my tremendous hubris to YouTube and surfed: here I found a video of a helpful stranger illustrating the secrets of unclogging a garbage disposal. I was mesmerized. I watched DIY videos and learned, knowing in my soul I could do anything.

The first project tackled was an easy one—re-cover the seats of our kitchen chairs. They were disgusting and cruddy with baby food splats, finger paint and red wine stains. Back at YouTube, E.J. and I learned how to unscrew the cushion from the chair base and using a flat-head screwdriver, wiggle out the existing staples. Peeling off the nasty and icky old cloth, we took a colorful cartoon-covered flat sheet from E.J.s' early years and meticulously measured and cut enough fabric to stretch over the cushion, wrapping the extra around the bottom of the wood base where we fastened the cloth, creating a sculpted fit. With both hands on my new industrial staple gun, I let it rip. *BOOM!* It was amazing! *BOOM!* It was thrilling! Thirty *BOOMS* later, the chair was gorgeous!

And so began my love affair with a staple gun. From my solar plexus, through my shoulder, down my arm and out my hand, I felt a surge of power that made me break out in a sweat. The gun offered both a hearty physical release and an immediate sense of completion. *I want more!* I said to myself.

That staple gun became the object of my desire. To thank my new community of caring neighbors for all their lawn support, I offered to re-cover kitchen chairs up and down the block. I went from being the wacky next-door neighbor to a superhero upholstering Rambo with a staple gun. *And I was good.*

By midsummer, after tackling many minor DIY projects around the house, I began to get itchy. There was one project calling me. It was the mother of all tasks—I wanted to re-screen our back porch!

E.J. and I both loved the back porch. We both decided that Fudgesicles tasted the best out there, eating them as we sat on a rusty antique glider. Rocking back and forth while we witnessed the end of another lazy summer day, we made up songs to go with the rhythm of the glider's squeaks. I gladly listened to my little girl's stories of who shared their Twizzlers or what boy splashed her in the pool. Then, as always, the creepy mosquitoes, flies and annoying no-see-ums would make their way through the gazillion rips and holes in the screens. We'd aimlessly swat and endlessly complain as we were chased inside, missing the magical transition of dusk turning into evening. We could have stayed out there forever.

I decided to keep this job simple. I would cough up the dough for the rolls of screen and a few wood nails, but the central character in this would be my beloved staple gun. I considered replacing the old shoe molding that framed the screen edges to the exterior porch walls, but I didn't want to buy new molding AND miter the corners of new molding AND paint new molding, so I thought to myself, *Screw new molding*. I just wanted to play with my staple gun and keep the bugs out.

I had some serious planning to do. By now, my buddies at the local hardware store adored me. I'd bring in fresh-baked goodies in exchange for their time and knowledge. They'd scurry to put on a fresh pot of coffee and we'd settle in for a schmooze, some treats, and a DIY lesson or two.

Rescreening an entire back porch was intimidating, so this particular store visit required something special. I prepared "Mandel Broit," a walnut and cinnamon eastern European biscotti, perfect for dunking. These über macho guys went crazy for these cookies and as they ate, they instructed me on the nuances in various types of screening and how to ensure a tight and lasting installation. I cherished their expertise and encouragement. With their stern warnings to measure twice and cut once, they sent me home, ready to fly solo. I knew I could do this, and like the Mandel Broit, *I'd be good!*

The next morning, I grabbed my daughter's ghetto blaster, plugged it in and cranked up the rock oldies station, ready to work. First, I gently guided the molding off the porch frame with a flat-head screwdriver and the claw side of a hammer. It was a delicate task—I needed to protect these tired old pieces of wood molding so they could be reused.

The hardware store guys suggested I recreate each screen window panel by laying the pieces of molding down on the driveway in the positions I took them from. This would help me remount them when all was said and done. Slowly, our driveway turned into what looked like six huge picture windows. E.J. went straight to work with her chalk, drawing people in the windows to wave and cheer me on. How could I not succeed with the support of an adoring 10-year-old and a 25-foot stretch of loving and positive green-and-purple chalk people?

E.J. ran off to play at a friend's house, just as I found myself physically and verbally arguing with the 500 rusty staples to be removed, but that wouldn't budge from the walls. With a mouth like a sailor and at my wits end, I stormed into the kitchen, grabbing the first pointy knife I saw. Back outside, I mercilessly dug under the obstinate staples, prying them from the wood so I could grab them with my pliers. I wiggled and yanked, sweating out every Fudgesicle I'd eaten that summer. Finally, two hours later, I knew the worst was over. The filthy and decrepit screens floated off the walls and I hurled them into the trash. Unrolling the new screen, I visualized summer nights sleeping on air mattresses with my daughter. With my own two hands, I was creating a wonderful place and like this wonderful place, *I was good*.

Loading my staple gun, I was almost breathless with anticipation, knowing I was moments away from the day's big pay-off. Stocked with an untold number of staples, I went around and around the six large screen panels, concentrating on each gratifying aim, squeeze and hit. I was forceful. *BOOM!* And loud. *BOOM!* And fast. *BOOM!* And I was yelling . . . *BOOM!* . . . and unaware . . . *BOOM!* . . . of my words, *BOOM!*

"Take that, you ex-husband you!" *BOOM!*

"Take that, you coffee shop owner who slipped me a Mocha Java when I specifically wanted plain coffee with soy milk. But nooooo, ya' wouldn't taste it and I looked like a fool!" *BOOM!*

"Take that, you little bully! I'm sorry your mother named you 'Clifford,' but that's no reason to wipe your boogers on my daughter!" *BOOM!*

And then it was over. The screens looked fabulous, tightly stretched and firmly secured to last another 70 years.

Suddenly, I was emotionally drained. This verbalizing had been aerobic, cathartic and therapeutic, leaving me with a euphoric and blinding buzz. I had to take a break and eat something huge and gross and unhealthy, and I had to eat it NOW. I drove to the one burger joint I would never take my child to. I ordered a cheeseburger, and not some junior cheeseburger or a weeny kids' meal, but a big-time-drippy-messy-get-it-on-your-pants-cheeseburger with fries, a Coke and a Tums. When I finished eating, it took all my strength to ignore the food coma that was draping over my eyes. I had to get the molding back up and I knew the afternoon would pass as quickly as the morning had.

Back at work, with the molding in one hand and a nail in

the other, I couldn't figure out how to bring the hammer into play. I needed three hands. How could I not have thought this through? It felt as though my delicious cheeseburger had rendered me stupid?

*What would my hardware boys do? Wait! Two-sided tape!* I'd been holding my life together with it for years and I had plenty. I stuck a lengthy piece of tape to the long stretch of molding, pressed the molding against the porch then set about hammering. *How smart is this, huh? I'm so good.*

I put a slew of nails between my lips and felt like a real carpenter. Between the vanilla lip-gloss with sunscreen and the metallic taste of the 2-inch nails, I was a diva-DIY woman, excited to get this porch finished.

Finally, the last piece of molding was nailed. I was done. My day was over and I closed my tool box. I stored the extra screen for whatever reason one keeps keeps extra screen, and then headed for a well-deserved shower.

Minutes later, E.J. came home, happy and hungry and proud of her mother's work. To celebrate, we ate our dinner out on the new and improved back porch. We sat on the glider with plates of pasta. I lit a few candles and we sang the song from *Lady and the Tramp* where the dogs' lips meet while eating the same spaghetti noodle. With plastic wine glasses full of grape juice, we drank a toast to the bugs who would never bug us again.

Marveling at the clean screens and spectacular view, I felt like a land baroness. I had committed to creating the perfect space for the two of us, and in doing so, I learned that with the help of great neighbors, terrific girlfriends, YouTube and a friendly hardware store, I would continue to kick some serious ass and get things done. It was thrilling to think that rather than nag, beg or hire, I could dream it, plan it, do it and ultimately, brag about it. It was then I realized that my daughter and I would be just fine.

And it was GOOD!

Sally holding E.J.

# NYMB Series Founders

Together, Dahlynn and Ken McKowen have 60-plus years of professional writing, editing, publication, marketing and public relations experience. Full-time authors and travel writers, the two have such a large body of freelance work that when they reached more than 2,000 articles, stories and photographs published, they stopped counting. And the McKowens are well-respected ghostwriters, having worked with CEOs and founders of some of the nation's biggest companies. They have even ghostwritten for a former U.S. president and a few California governors and elected officials.

From 1999 to 2009, Ken and Dahlynn were consultants and coauthors for *Chicken Soup for the Soul*, where they collaborated with series founders Jack Canfield and Mark Victor Hansen on several books such as *Chicken Soup for the Entrepreneur's Soul; Chicken Soup for the Soul in Menopause; Chicken Soup for the Fisherman's Soul;* and *Chicken Soup for the Soul: Celebrating Brothers and Sisters*. They also edited and ghost-created many more Chicken titles during their tenure, with Dahlynn reading more than 100,000 story submissions.

For highly acclaimed outdoor publisher Wilderness Press, the McKowens' books include *Best of Oregon and Washington's Mansions, Museums and More; The Wine-Oh! Guide to California's Sierra Foothills* and national award-winning *Best of California's Missions, Mansions and Museums*.

Under Publishing Syndicate, the couple authored and published *Wine Wherever: In California's Mid-Coast & Inland*

*Region*, and are actively researching wineries for *Wine Wherever: In California's Paso Robles Region*, the second book in the Wine Wherever series.

If that's not enough, the McKowens are also the creators of the Wine Wherever iPhone mobile winery-destination journaling app and are currently creating a travel television show under the same brand (www.WineWherever.com).

Dahlynn and Ken relaxing in their backyard

The McKowens' latest DIY project—a chicken coop

# NYMB Co-Creator

## About Pamela Frost

Born with a silver spoon in her mouth? Not Pamela Frost—she probably had a screwdriver. As the self-proclaimed "Queen of the Do-it-Yourselfers," Pamela—aka Handy Pammy—would rather browse the aisles of Home Depot than Neiman Marcus. She's in love with her Fein MultiMaster.

When she was much younger, she told her father she wanted to be a painter and live in a Paris loft. He put a roller in her hand and told her to paint her bedroom, and then they changed the oil in the car. Born in Cleveland, Ohio to a working class family, money was always tight. That changes a girl. Pamela is a different kind of woman and proud of it.

Pamela's first real job was as a telephone operator for GTE. It was the 1970s, a time of affirmative action. She was encouraged to bid on a job as a central office installer and got it. Being one of the first women to break into the trades was not easy, but her I-can-do-anything attitude and being a quick learner carried her through. Later, Pamela became the first female licensed independent electrical contractor in the city of Cleveland.

She bought her first house when she was just 22—of course, it was a fixer-upper. Through trial and error, Pamela learned to do everything from plumbing to laying tile. At the tender age of 41, she convinced her reluctant husband to flip houses. She argued she had all the skills necessary to get rich in real estate, having completed three house renovations up to that point. Tutoring her then 14-year-old son, Chris, his friends, and her husband in the fine art of demolition and restoration, they built their business. In eight years, they renovated 12 houses, while managing the rentals. Pamela writes about their hilarious misadventures in landlord-land in her award-winning novel, *Houses of Cards*.

Pamela did not get rich. She did, however, get divorced.

Pamela currently lives in Medina, Ohio and is now married to her soul mate.

Look for Pamela's short stories in other *Not Your Mother's Book* titles, as well as *Cup of Comfort for Mothers and Daughters*.

Pam cleans up nicely!

# Contributor Bios

**Banjo Bandolas'** stories have appeared in local, national and international publications. His style of storytelling reflects his Southern roots. Previous anthologies include numerous *Chicken Soup* books and *Oregon Ghost Story* compilations. He works as a globe-trotting beer writer for Realbeer.com. (You heard right—he gets paid to travel and drink beer!)

**Beth Bartlett** is a freelance writer and humorist in northwest Arkansas. Her work has appeared in numerous publications, and her newspaper column, "Wisecrack Zodiac," won an award in the humor category of the 2013 National Society of Newspaper Columnists competition. Connect with her on Twitter @plaidearthworm.

**Heidi Griminger Blanke,** Ph.D., lives in La Crosse, Wisconsin. She writes regularly for two regional magazines and has published several humor essays, including on the Erma Bombeck Writers' Workshop website. She is currently penning a series of humorous essays about menopause. Blanke also volunteers her writing skills with several nonprofit agencies.

**Arthur Bowler,** a U.S./Swiss citizen and graduate of Harvard Divinity School, is a writer, speaker and minister of English and German. He is currently seeking representation for his book, *A Prayer and a Swear*. Contact www.arthurbowler.ch or bowler@bluewin.ch.

**Debra Ayers Brown** is a creative nonfiction writer, blogger, magazine humor columnist and award-winning marketing professional. Enjoy her stories in other *Not Your Mother's Books, Chicken Soup for the Soul, Guideposts, Woman's World* and more. Connect with her at www.About.Me/DebraAyersBrown.

**Kathe Campbell** lives her dream on a Montana mountain with her mammoth donkeys, a Keeshond and a few kitties. Three children, 11 grandkids, and four greats round out the herd. She is a prolific writer on Alzheimer's and a contributing author to the *Chicken Soup for the Soul* series, medical journals and magazines.

**Kari Lynn Collins** lives in Wichita Falls, Texas and works for a weekly newspaper, the *Iowa Park Leader*. She also authors two blogs, "That's What She Says" and "Power of B.O.B.," which can be found at www.karilynncollins.com.

**Harriet Cooper** is a freelance writer and has published personal essays, humor and creative nonfiction in newspapers, newsletters, anthologies and magazines. She writes about family, relationships, health, food, cats and daily life. She is currently working on a humorous book about lessons her cats have taught her. Email: shewrites@live.ca.

**Shari Courter** is married to her high school sweetheart, Ron, and they have four children: Zac, Aubrey, Kearstin and Caymen. Shari is a licensed massage therapist and stay-at-home mom. In her spare time, she enjoys *not* doing yardwork and blogging about her family's antics.

**Kathryn Cureton** writes from the basement lair of her hillbilly mansion in southeast Missouri. She makes a living teaching high school science. Her hobbies include bragging that she graduated valedictorian, keeping her husband from using the front yard sinkhole as nature's giant wastebasket and using prepositions to end sentences with.

**Terri Duncan,** a high school administrator, is a devoted wife and mother of two grown children. She hopes they support her in her retirement so she can pursue her dream of writing. She has authored numerous short stories and published *Camping Reservations: Body of Lies*, a book for young readers.

**Terri Elders**, a lifelong freelance writer and editor, has published stories in over 75 anthologies since she retired to northeast Washington with her late husband, Ken Wilson, in 2004. She is a public member of the Washington Medical Quality Assurance Commission and a co-creator and copyeditor for the *Not Your Mother's Book* series.

**Stephanie Fellenstein** is an award-winning journalist from Aurora, Ohio. She spends most of her time trying to stay one step ahead of her husband, two daughters, a dog, cats, goats and turtle. Unfortunately, it is a losing battle.

**Sally Fingerett**, of The Four Bitchin' Babes musical comedy theater group, has released five solo CDs. Her song *Home Is Where the Heart Is* has been recorded by Peter, Paul and Mary. Her lyrics and prose are included in Random House's *Life's a Stitch* collection of contemporary women's humor. www.sallyfingerett.com

**Monica Giglio**'s stories have been read around the world, as well as in a local news magazine in Warren, New Jersey where she lives. She's also a nationally known fine artist with work oversees in the federal Arts in Embassies program. She is the founder of Purpose Driven Arts and can be reached at monica@monicagiglio.com.

**Dianna Graveman** is a writer, editor and designer with over 160 published pieces and co-authorship of four regional histories. She is founder of 2 Rivers Communications & Design, LLC and a partner at Treehouse Publishing Group, LLC. Visit her at www.2riverscommunications.com and www.treehousepublishinggroup.com.

**Abigail Green** has published over 200 articles and essays in various magazines, anthologies and websites. She is also the author of the e-book *Mama Insider: Laughing (And Sometimes Crying) All the Way Through Pregnancy, Birth, and the First 3 Months*, available on Amazon. She lives in Baltimore with her family.

**Stacey Gustafson** has a humor column called "Are You Kidding Me?" based on her suburban family and everyday life. Her stories have appeared in *Chicken Soup for the Soul: The Magic of Mothers and Daughters* and *Not Your Mother's Book...On Being a Woman, On Travel* and *On Being a Parent*. Blog: www.staceygustafson.com.

**Cathy C. Hall** is a humor writer from the warm and wonderful South. She's published in both adult and children's markets, in fiction and nonfiction. See what she's working on now at www.c-c-hall.com.

**Sheila S. Hudson** appears in *Chocolate for Women, Chicken Soup, Patchwork Path, Love Story 1&2*, plus numerous periodicals. Her byline is also in *Purple Pros* and *Costumer Magazine*. She established Bright Ideas to bring hope and inspiration through the written word. Sheila served as president of Southeastern Writers Association. sheilahudson.writer@gmail.com http://sh5633.wix.com/13decisions.

**Cindy Hval** is a columnist for the *Spokesman Review* newspaper in Spokane, Washington where she lives with her husband, four sons and two cats. Her stories have been published in numerous anthologies. She's currently working on her first book: *War Bonds: Love Stories From the Greatest Generation*.

**Caroleah Johnson** is a retired dental hygienist, currently working as a health coach, cooking instructor and personal chef. In her limited free time, she raises organic vegetables, writes nonfiction and sews for her grandchildren. She lives in California's northern Sierra foothills where she has endless opportunities for DIY projects.

**Janet Sheppard Kelleher** is editing a collection of down-home Southern stories with the same name as her newspaper column, "Havin' My Cotton-Pickin' Say." A long-term breast cancer survivor, Janet is also polishing a humorous how-to-cope book called *Big C, Little Ta-Tas*. Look for both books in 2014.

**Cindy Kloosterman** lives in the small town of Shelby, North Carolina. She has three children and worked as a nurse for 25 years before returning to her first love—writing. She loves creating things for her home, although she would be the first to admit they're not always perfect.

**Gloria Hander Lyons** has channeled 35 years of training and hands-on experience in the areas of art, interior decorating, crafting, event planning and self-publishing into writing creative how-to books, fun cookbooks and humorous slice-of-life stories. Visit her website to read about them all: www.gloriahanderlyons.com.

**Meg Mardis** and her not-so-handy, but precious, husband live in an A-frame in the woods of Randolph, Ohio. At work, she writes for trade, peer-reviewed and consumer publications and is an award-winning marketer. A member of Sisters in Crime, Meg is putting finishing touches on an amateur sleuth medical mystery.

**David Martin**'s humor and political satire have appeared in many publications including *The New York Times*, the *Chicago Tribune* and *Smithsonian Magazine*. His latest humor collection *Screams & Whispers* is available on Amazon.com. David lives in Ottawa, Canada with his wife, Cheryl, and their daughter, Sarah.

**Timothy Martin** is the author of *Summer With Dad*, *Rez Rock*, and *Wimps Like Me*. Timothy has completed nine screenplays, two TV pilots and has two books due out in 2013: *Fast Pitch* and *Somewhere Down The Line*. He has done commentary on National Public Radio. Timothy can be reached at tmartin@northcoast.com.

**Laurel (Bernier) McHargue** was raised as "Daughter #4" of five girls in Braintree, Massachusetts where she lived until heading to Smith College, followed by the United States Military Academy. Her constant quest for adventure landed her in Leadville, Colorado where she currently resides with her husband. Visit her at www.leadvillelaurel.com.

**Mike McHugh** is author of "The Dang Yankee," a humorous column about life in Louisiana and the world at large from the perspective of a slowly graying Northerner who never quite grew up. Started in 2009, it's a popular feature in *The Louisiana Jam*, a publication covering southwest Louisiana and southeast Texas.

**Mary Mendoza**, known to fans as "Madcap," is the author of four humor collections based on her zany escapades. She writes "Udder Nonsense" for *Country Pleasures* magazine and hosts a blog at madcapmary.wordpress.com. An *Auntie Mame* devotee and irrepressible bon vivant, she hopes to one day run in the Kentucky Derby.

**Lesley Morgan** is an art educator, visual artist and author who isn't afraid to get her hands dirty. Written works previously published include poems and work-related nonfiction. She lives near the New Hampshire seacoast.

**Alice Muschany** lives in Flint Hill, Missouri. Recently retired, she's having trouble figuring out why she still can't find time to clean. Meanwhile, she's busy enjoying her grandchildren, hiking, biking, taking pictures and writing essays. Life is good!

**MaryAnn Myers** is the bestselling author of the *Thoroughbred Racetrack* novels *Favored to Win, Odds on Favorite, and Barn 14—Meg's Meadows of the Winning Odds Series*. A thoroughbred owner and racehorse fan, she lives on an organic farm in northeast Ohio with her husband and a menagerie of animals.

**Pat Nelson**—a writer and editor—is co-creator of *NYMB...On Being a Parent* and two upcoming NYMB titles: *On Being a Grandparent* and *On Working for a Living*. Her stories appear at www.LewisRiver.com and she blogs at www.storystorm.me. Nelson is writing a nonfiction book about a tuberculosis sanatorium in northern Minnesota.

**Tori Nichols** is a writer-poet and a proud do-it-yourselfer born of necessity, sustained by desire. She has attended the Handywoman's School of Hard Knocks where she learned that the theory of "tuck and roll" is a philosophy that can be applied to all aspects of life. Message her at www.torinichols.com.

**Risa Nye** lives in Oakland, California. She co-edited *Writin' on Empty* (available on Amazon and Kindle). Her articles and essays have appeared in local and national publications and in several anthologies. She writes about the craft of nonfiction for Hippocampus magazine. Her "Ms. Barstool" cocktail column appears online at Berkeleyside.com.

**Linda O'Connell**—a seasoned teacher from St. Louis, Missouri—enjoys a good book, a hearty laugh, long walks on the beach and dark chocolate. She is a multi-published writer and co-creator of *Not Your Mother's Book...On Family.*

**Suzanne Olsen** lives in Portland, Oregon. Her humor essays have been published in *The Oregonian* newspaper. She's co-written articles about solar energy for Home Power magazine, and edited the book *Footprint, A Funny Thing Happened on the Way to Extinction* about global warming. Her website and blog are at www.gentlehumor.com.

**Lucia Paul**'s humor writing includes an award-winning sitcom script and essays that have appeared in numerous publications. Her parody "Fifty Shades of Flannel" (under the pen name Nancy O'Toole) was an *Entertainment Weekly* editor's pick in 2012. Her book *Home Buyers Just Aren't That Into You* is due out in 2013.

**Jill Pertler** touches hearts and funny bones with her weekly syndicated column, "Slices of Life," printed in 130 newspapers across the U.S. She is a playwright, author of *The Do-it-Yourselfer's Guide to Self-Syndication* and has stories published in three *Chicken Soup* books. Follow the "Slices of Life" page on Facebook.

**Cappy Hall Rearick** is a syndicated newspaper columnist, an award-winning short-story writer and author of six books and five successful columns. Featured by the Erma Bombeck Writers' Workshop as a Humor Writer of the Month, Rearick's humor and short fiction has been read and enjoyed in anthologies throughout the country.

**John Reas** is excited to continue to express himself through his writing and the NYMB series. This marks his fourth story in the NYMB family. And yes, he has a very patient wife when it comes to his handyman skills!

**Maureen Rogers** is a Canadian transplant living in Seattle, Washington. Her essays and fiction have appeared in many online and print publications including five *Chicken Soup for the Soul* anthologies and *Not Your Mothers Book...On Being a Parent.* Her current project is a short story collection: *Hose Jockeys, Hotshots and Heroes.* Contact: morogers@gmail.com

**John Schlimm** is an activist, artist, educator and the international award-winning author of such books as *Stand Up!: 75 Young Activists Who Rock the World, And How You Can, Too!; The Cheesy Vegan; Grilling Vegan Style; The Tipsy Vegan* and several others. For more information, please visit www.JohnSchlimm.com.

**Maggie Lamond Simone** is a national award-winning columnist. Her books include *From Beer to Maternity* and *POSTED!*, and she has essays in *P.S. What I Didn't Say* and multiple *Chicken Soup for the Soul* editions. She teaches journalism at SUNY Oswego, Oswego, New York and blogs for *The Huffington Post*.

**Bobby Barbara Smith** lives in Bull Shoals, Arkansas. Her humorous, heartfelt short stories have been published in *Not Your Mother's Book...On Dogs* and *Not Your Mother's Book...On Being a Stupid Kid*, plus in other anthologies and e-zines.

**Susan Swartwout** is professor of English at Southeast Missouri State University, founder and publisher of the University Press and editor of journals *Big Muddy* and *The Cape Rock: Poetry*. She has six published books and over 100 poems and essays in anthologies, collections and literary magazines.

**Judi Tepe** has been a guest columnist for the *Illinois Sun Day*. Her column, "A Slice of Life," is a peek into the lives of the folks who live in these communities and consider themselves too young to retire and too old to move quickly and without pain. Email: juditepe@gmail.com.

**Camille DeFer Thompson** lives in Northern California and has been writing since childhood. She has won acclaim for her fiction and nonfiction published in a number of anthologies. Her feature articles appear online and in print. Camille's brief foray into home repair has fostered a renewed respect for live current.

**Lisa Tognola**, also known as "Jersey Girl," highlights the humorous side of suburban life—the good, the bad and the ugly—in her blog Mainstreetmusingsblog. com. She is a contributor to the humor anthologies *My Funny Valentine* and *My Funny Medical*, and the online magazine More.com. Twitter @lisatognola.

**Pat Wahler** is a freelance writer in Missouri. She is a grant writer by day and writer of essays and fiction by night. Her work has been published in numerous local and national venues. A lifelong animal lover, Pat ponders critters, writing and life's little mysteries at www.critteralley.blogspot.com.

**Tracy Winslow** is a SAHM trying not to raise a flock of assholes. Besides crafting cocktails with Zoloft, Tracy can be found cursing, crying into her coffee over her stretch marks and Ouija-boarding her deceased metabolism. When she's not wrangling children and small animals, she is blogging at http://www.momaical.com.

**Dianne J. Wilson** lives in East London, South Africa. She's been freelance writing for magazines since 2004, in between making sure her three kids are mostly clean and don't starve. A firm believer that every situation has a funny side, laughing at life has become a habit far cheaper than drugs.

**Ernie Witham** writes the nationally syndicated column "Ernie's World" for the *Montecito Journal* in Santa Barbara, California. He is also the author of two humor books and leads humor writing workshops in several cities. Ernie is on the permanent faculty of the Santa Barbara Writers Conference.

# Story Permissions

*The Domino Effect* © 2004 Joseph Bandolas
*Stick-to-itiveness* © 2010 Beth Bartlett
*It Looked So Easy* © 2013 Heidi Griminger Blanke
*Euro Shock* © 2013 Arthur Wilson Bowler
*Power Play* © 2013 Debra Brown
*Flood or Fame* © 2010 Kathleen M. Campbell
*The Formation of Death* © 2012 Kari Lynn Collins
*Nice Try* © 2013 Harriet Cooper
*Thou Shalt Not* © 2010 Shari Courter
*Plier-Lamping 101* © 2005 Kathryn Cureton
*Coming Unglued* © 2012 Terri Duncan
*Deep Doo Doo* © 2012 Terri Duncan
*A Zillion Zinnias* © 2008 Theresa J. Elders
*Muddy Waters* © 2013 Stephanie J. Fellenstein
*It's All Good* © 2013 Sally Fingerett
*Caribbean Blue* © 2008 Pamela Frost
*It Hits the Fan* © 2012 Pamela Frost
*What Comes Around Goes Around* © 2007 Pamela Frost
*Reverse-Engineering* © 2013 Monica Giglio
*Rooftop Free-fall* © 2012 Dianna Graveman
*Pinterest Made Me Do It* © 2012 Abigail Green Forhan
*He's Not That Into Me* © 2012 Stacey Gustafson
*He Who Kills Weeds* © 2013 Stacey Gustafson
*A Handywoman's Tale* © 2013 Cathy C. Hall
*Kill a Watt?* © 2003 Sheila S. Hudson
*Monument to Manhood* © 2006 Cindy Hval
*Fuzzy Logic* © 2013 Caroleah Johnson
*Even if Askew* © 2013 Janet Sheppard Kelleher
*Let's Get Crafty* © 2012 Cindy Kloosterman
*In Hot Water* © 2011 Gloria Hander Lyons
*The Missing Gene* © 2013 Meg Mardis
*A DIY GPS* © 2010 David Joseph Martin
*The Powderless Powder Room* © 2011 David Joseph Martin
*In Pursuit of Perfection* © 2005 Timothy Lee Martin
*Lines and Lions* © 2013 Laurel J. McHargue
*Awl in the Family* © 2013 John Michael McHugh
*Fan-dango* © 2013 John Michael McHugh
*The Perils of Paint* © 2003 Mary F. Mendoza
*Steamed* © 2009 Lesley Morgan
*It Had to Be Yew* © 2008 Lesley Morgan

# Publishing Syndicate

Publishing Syndicate LLC is an independent book publisher based in Northern California. The company has been in business for more than a decade, mainly providing writing, ghostwriting and editing services for major publishers. In 2011, Publishing Syndicate took the next step and expanded into a full-service publishing house.

The company is owned by married couple Dahlynn and Ken McKowen. Dahlynn is the CEO and publisher, and Ken serves as president and managing editor.

Publishing Syndicate's mission is to help writers and authors realize personal success in the publishing industry, and, at the same time, provide an entertaining reading experience for its customers. From hands-on book consultation and their very popular and free monthly *Wow Principles* publishing tips e-newsletter to forging book deals with both new and experienced authors and launching three new anthology series, Publishing Syndicate has created a powerful and enriching environment for those who want to share their writing with the world. (www.PublishingSyndicate.com)

# NYMB Needs Your Stories!

We are looking for hip, fun, modern and very-much-today stories, just like those in this book, for 30 new titles in the *NYMB* series. Published contributors are compensated.

**Submission guidelines at www.PublishingSyndicate.com**